Cover and book design: Studio 3, Ellsworth, Maine
Printed by The Ellsworth American, Ellsworth, Maine USA

(ISBN 0-9639070-0-X)

Published by

Dilligaf©
P U B L I S H I N G

64 Court Street, Ellsworth, Maine 04605

Funny, you don't look

CRAZY

Life with obsessive-compulsive disorder.

Constance H. Foster

This work is dedicated to:

My husband, Stephen, who has so lovingly and thoroughly convinced me that our life together has been, is, and will continue to be so worthwhile, despite it all.

My beautiful and brave sons: Christopher, Jesse and Nicholas, who have shown a maturity and understanding beyond their young years in always knowing the difference between Mom and Mom's Brain Cramps.

My Mom and Dad, with love and thanks, for also passing along those great genes that have made it possible for me to do this project.

Fran and Ma P., who flew without wings many years ago, for their courage, strength and bad jokes.

Terry, who, like me, often leaves her vac double parked and running.

Dr. S. R., who unknowingly gave me the seed of an idea for this book, not to mention the title.

And last of all, but most importantly, to all of you courageous people out there with OCD who spend a good part of every day feeling as if you're working without the safety net.

A TRULY SPECIAL DEDICATION OF THIS BOOK IS MADE
TO THE MEMORY OF
MONICA JEAN PRIME

BLACK TIDES OF LONELINESS

Wash over and around my being;
Sometimes nearly swamping my
Fragile barque in an evil sea.
Sometimes bringing me a short-term death.

But my isolation is nothing
When seen beside her
Painful exile, her enforced quarantine.
Nothing when I remember her
Terrible estrangement, a child apart.
She walked the path of solitude,
Exclusion, alienation, and oblivion.

A terrible sentence where only death
Brought more than piecemeal peace.

Ralph R. Prime

FUNNY, YOU DON'T LOOK CRAZY
Life with Obsessive-Compulsive Disorder

FOREWARD

"WHAT ARE YOUR TOUCHING TREES?"

Good Question! I've worked hard to give up my Touching Trees since OCD struck me in 1982. So what is a Touching Tree? It's a metaphor for something we give power to that really doesn't have that kind of power. In our film *The Touching Tree*, a child of 10 who is afflicted with OCD becomes stuck in a "counting ritual" at a huge tree on a school playground. From this OCD experience he becomes terrified of the tree. He avoids it, becomes phobic around it, in essence gives it power it really doesn't have. How many times in my life with OCD have I given things power they don't have? From magical germs on door knobs, keys, bathroom appliances, to thinking I could actually have the power to harm someone from my thoughts. So what's the answer to all this Touching Tree business? For me it's been a combination of medication, behavior therapy, cognitive therapy, and support groups. I believe that last one is crucial for us. We need not suffer alone. The best way I've been taught to take my power back is to go through the fear, as opposed to all the things we do to avoid the fear, whatever the fear may be, and practice, practice, practice. By going through fears, you find out at a very deep level that the world just doesn't operate the way our OCD thinking thinks. This is a tough road to walk but it doesn't have to happen all at once and you don't have to take on all your fears. It's a process. I've actually worked at NOT being perfect at this process. Remember, it's "Progress, not perfection" we're after.

Becoming more aware of your "Touching Trees" is a wonderful start to recovery. With the proper support from therapists, family, friends and support groups, like Terry in *The Touching Tree*, you can take your power back and find out that a Touching Tree is just a tree.

by James Callner
Writer/Director of *The Touching Tree*

PREFACE

"When you arrive at a fork in the road, take it."

Yogi Berra

Recently, a well-published author told me that I should "write as if it were being read by intelligent people." So, if you're not, put this book down...right now.

Although I do hate to start off by making your eyes glaze over, current statistics do tell us there are literally millions of Americans out there with Obsessive-Compulsive Disorder. One out of every fifty adults, to be more exact. This figure does not even begin to encompass the rest of the world's population. Just think of it, millions of people who struggle with their disease every day just like you and I do! So, okay, I give up! Where are you all hiding? But even as I ask that question, I know the answer. You've all concealed your OCD well, just as I have, for so long. Well, I've decided that I am tired of and finished with trying to disguise something that isn't my fault! Honestly, it's true...I did not get up one morning, turn to my husband and say, "You know what, Hon? Things are a bit slow at the moment and I could really use a good case of OCD right now to stir things up." Obsessive-Compulsive Disorder is a disease that can sneak right up on you when you're not looking. Then, before you know it, BANG! right between the eyes! All of a sudden, you and your family are living and dancing as fast as you can daily, just to keep a solid grip on everything.

That is the reason for this book. I have made a decision to no longer hide from, apologize for, or feel ashamed because of a physical condition that I did not ask to have. This book is not a medical or clinical text; nor is it one of those dreaded "How To" books. Every person who suffers with OCD has their own unique obsessions and complusions, simply because everyone's brain chemicals are also uniquely their own. Consequently, I would not presume to tell anyone how they should cope with their disease. You will not find a "cure" in these pages, as I certainly have no magic answers.

There is really only one thing that I am certain of. Sometimes, not everything can be "fixed", either in part or entirely. Where does that leave us? In the end, after all the anger, rage, bewilderment, confusion, frustration, guilt, and tears, there is really no alternative but to just get on with it and somehow try to find some sort of balance within ourselves that allows us, in each our own way, to somehow work our lives around this devastating disease. This book then, is for all of us and also, for the people we love and who love us in return. As I have said, you won't find any magical answers among these pages. Just some very personal accounts of a few of us who, like you, have this disease and yet, despite this... or could it really be because of our daily pain, we are still able to find the joy in living.

"Experience is not what happens to you, but what you do with what happens to you."

Aldous Huxley

"Plainly, the fear of insanity, hypnotically working on his imagination, had mounted to such a degree that he finally, in exhausted despair, bought the fetters and padlocks lest the enemy that seemed to be winning against him pass beyond control."

Samuel Johnson
By Walter Jackson Bates

WHAT IS OBSESSIVE-COMPULSIVE DISORDER?

Obsessive-Compulsive Disorder is a neurological illness that traps people who have it into almost endless cycles of repetitive thoughts that won't leave their minds (called obsessions) and incredibly strong feelings that they must repeat certain actions, or rituals, over and over again (called compulsions).

Those of us who suffer from obsessions, no matter how senseless the obsession may be, try to ignore or suppress it, but we can't. Obsessions may be unpleasant, frightening, distasteful, or even, sometimes, repugnant. They may occur only so often or infrequently, but, in most cases, they are almost constant. Typically, the obsessions cause, not just a touch of small annoyance, but very real and severe anxiety.

Feelings of fear, panic, dread, and discomfort can, and will, build up to an unbearable level. This is when the compulsive act or acts enter into it. These are designed to relieve or prevent some danger or harm that could happen either to ourselves or to someone else. The anxiety level can become so high that, in order to relieve it, you must act...you must do something.

Generally, these actions or rituals must be performed according to certain rules. Sometimes these rituals are fairly simple and therefore, difficult, even tricky, for others to notice. But, more commonly, they tend to be extremely elaborate. In fact, they are usually so complex that your entire lifestyle is interfered with. Rituals can be incredibly time consuming, sometimes, for some of us, taking hours every single day to complete. For some of us these rituals can be terribly exhausting. However, they do provide some sort of relief from the more immediate feelings of anxiety, discomfort or disgust, but (and here is the "Catch 22"), only for a very brief time. The worries, fears and tensions will soon return, and the rituals will start all over again.

There are many different types of obsessions and compulsions. They are as varied as those of us who experience them. Just a very brief description of a few of the so-called "typical" obsessions and compulsions are as follows:
FEAR OF CONTAMINATION:
Extreme horror of dirt and/or germs, either on oneself or just in one's en-

vironment. These fears usually involve repeated rituals of handwashing, showering, or cleaning. Sometimes, the skin is washed so often that it may become raw and red. Other people may feel the overpowering need to keep their homes so spotless that virtually hours are spent every day polishing, scrubbing, vacuuming, only to clean the entire house again, if someone drops by for a visit. That, of course, is assuming that they can comfortably invite people into their homes.

CHECKING:

Although "doubt" is very strong in all individuals with OCD, it is particularly overwhelming in those with a checking compulsion. When this compulsion is involved, logic, reassurance from others, or just plain common sense cannot always be trusted. Each of us at one time or another has had the feeling that we've forgotten something important or left the iron plugged in when rushing off to work in the morning. But if you are a checker, you will not go back to check just once. You will constantly check and re-check to make sure that lights are out, doors and windows are locked, and appliances turned off. There are times that some individuals are able to "borrow" a trusted person's knowledge. For example, a child may frequently wake his parents at night in order to re-check certain things in the house. People who are checkers, more than with most of the other compulsions, seem to have lost their ability to "know" that everything is all right, in its proper place and locked or switched off. Even though their eyes can see this, somehow the knowledge of really "knowing" is short-circuited out somewhere in the brain. These compulsions make many tasks, no matter how simple, take hours to finish. For example, school work must be gone back over again and again. These efforts are so terribly time-consuming that often children have fallen far behind in school and adults have been fired from their work, or, in some cases, have simply given up trying to stay on top of it all and quit.

COUNTING/REPEATING:

People whose compulsion is to count are easily involved in hours of counting everything they may come across...cars driving by, people walking on the street, or even just how many times one breathes in and out, or snaps their chewing gum. Sometimes, people who count must reach a certain number before a task can feel totally complete to them or safe to stop. Sometimes, certain motions, such as rising from a chair, must be repeated a certain "magical" number of times. Words sometimes must be repeated, as in a mantra, to protect ourselves or someone that we love from harm.

HOARDING:

A good many people are "collectors" who take great satisfaction and joy in their area of interest, whether it be antiques, rare books, fine art, stamps, or magic nose goblins. But, when a person with OCD is a collector, they are totally unable to part with or throw away anything, even items that would be of absolutely no value to the local junkman. Eventually, those of us with this compulsion have every room in the house or apartment totally overrun with collections" of everything imaginable, from small bits of yarn to discarded slips of unimportant papers picked up from the streets.

STRANGE MOVEMENTS:

There are some rituals that can take the form of odd movements, such as jumping upwards to touch a door frame so many times, or having a specific number of times one must turn around before being able to pass through a doorway. Some people with this compulsion may walk in such a way as to use strange steps, skips, leaps, or jumps, not to mention unusual arm or body movements. This type of compulsion is very mindful of Monty Python's classic "Ministry of Odd Walks" film. Remember the old nursery rhyme about being cautioned to "never step on a crack or you could break your mother's back?" This can be taken very seriously, indeed, if your compulsion is odd and strange movements.

TRICHOTILLOMANIA:

This is a compulsion to pull out one's body hair. Those of us who have this compulsion don't go outside on windy and blustery days, ride in cherry-red Mustangs with the tops down, go swimming, or get caught in torrential rain storms. Your arms can, literally, be sore and ache from hours of hair pulling. Trichotillomania is very different from all other types of obsessions and compulsions in that the overwhelming majority of those of us who have it tend to be female, although males are certainly still susceptible to this symptom as well.

RELIGIOUS SCRUPULOSITY:

Imagine always trying to cut a better deal with God? Those of us who have religious scrupulosity are constantly barraged with obsessive thoughts...day and night. This is one of the more exhausting manifestations of OCD as you can't "escape" from your thoughts, no matter how hard you try. Often, scrupulosity is tied up with "harmful" thoughts. For example, if I am sure to pray just the correct way, this many times a day, then no harm will befall the people that I know and/or love.

As diverse as all of these obsessions and compulsions are, it is quite common for someone with OCD to have a combination of several of them. Sometimes, one or more may take over and become totally all-important for a length of time, only to be replaced by something different...a brand new twist, after one week, six months, or fifty-two years.

As I stated earlier in this chapter, this is meant to be only a very partial listing of the more "typical" obsessions and compulsions to be found in those of us who suffer with OCD. Those of you who may be interested in a much broader scope of this subject (such as more depth on the medical aspect), will find a, hopefully helpful, suggested reading and reference list towards the back of this book.

There are many theories about how one "gets" OCD. They seem to be almost as endless as the rituals. As most of the research on OCD is still relatively new, there really aren't that many facts available right now. One bit of information, however, that is a solid fact, is that this is a biological disease, somehow caused by a malfunction of some sort in the brain's circuitry.

In working theories at the moment, top considerations are: genetics; serotonin (brain chemical); neurons (brain cells); glial cells (these are the support cells for the neurons); stress; trauma; and other neurological injury or disease.

Serotonin, put simply, regulates our brain function, acting as an inhibitor by way of preventing an excess of neuron firing. One of the characteristics of serotonin that makes it a bit different from our other brain chemicals, is that serotonin neurons control a rather large area of the functioning of our brains. If your serotonin, neurons and/or glial cells are malfunctioning at all, then your brain and the message it sends out to the rest of your body is being short-circuited, not unlike an electric cord that is badly frayed.

Genetics play an extremely important role, as statistics state that about 20% of us with OCD come from a family in which another close family member also suffers with it. (Personally, I feel that this percentage is way off; a more realistic figure would be much higher.) What is different, however, is that the chances are that you and your relative will not have the same type of obsessions and compulsions. For example, if your mother is a "hoarder" you could very well be a "cleaner". Apparently, what is passed down from one generation to the next, is a tendency for the neurons to become more easily damaged in those of us with this disease than in other people. Therefore, there is the ability to develop OCD under just the right circumstances, such as monumental stress, trauma, or contracting another neurological disease that also affects our neurotransmitters.

Whatever the reason for OCD, it is certainly not a rare disease, as was once thought. As a matter of fact, judging from current statistics (1 out of every 50 adults), I would say it is fairly common, much more so than most of us are aware. OCD can and does affect all ages...adults, teens and young children. Aside from being non-discriminatory about age, this disease does not care how you are fixed economically or what your social standing is in the local community.

If you have obsessive-compulsive disease, then you have an illness that you need to try to have treated just as you would any other physical illness.

"And how many hours a day did you do lessons?" said Alice.
"Ten hours the first day," said the Mock Turtle, "nine the next, and so on."
"What a curious plan!" exclaimed Alice.
"That's the reason they're called lessons," the Gryphon remarked: "because they lessen from day to day."

Alice's Adventures in Wonderland
Lewis Carroll

At this time the options that are available to choose from to help treat OCD are fairly limited. There are a few neurological drugs (specifically geared towards serotonin re-uptake) that have shown to be rather successful for some people. Still others have found some relief from a combination of medications and behavioral therapy (rather like trying to "re-train" the brain). Some people with this disease have found the "Twelve Steps" programs to be useful. Also, there are those who have found the "A + T" therapy (Acetazolamide and Thiamine) developed by Dr. Aristide Esser and Dr. William Sacks at the Nathan Kline Institute in 1985 to have been indispensable to a successful treatment. Rather than focussing only on the nerve endings, "A + T" zeros in on making the changes within the brain cells themselves by replenishing the enzymes that are crucial to keeping chemical messages between the brain cells unimpaired.

But still, despite all the recent advancements in research for OCD, there are still a good number of us who have not been able to find an answer yet. Our only alternative, until that fantastic day arrives for each of us who are victims of this disease, is to have a great anticipation for the future and to hope that, in the meantime, people will be, if not understanding, at least non-judgemental.

"Well, now that we have seen each other," said the Unicorn, "if you believe in me, I'll believe in you..."

Lewis Carroll

"I've had nothing yet," Alice replied in an offended tone, *"so I can't take more."*

"You mean you can't take less," said the Hatter: *"It's very easy to take more than less."*

Lewis Carroll

OBSESSIVE-COMPULSIVE DISORDER AND GENETICS

Without exception, each and every one of us has, within our bodies, defective and abnormal genes. As of today, it is largely left up to fate as to if and when these genes are moved along the hereditary track.

This entire school of thought brings us into the subject area of human genetics, or, more accurately, eugenics. Defined, eugenics is the attempt to improve a population through selective breeding—the genetic engineering of specific, particular human qualities.

The genetics movement began in England with Sir Francis Galton, who happened to also be a cousin of Charles Darwin. Galton believed in the so-called "eminence" of members of the aristocracy through a particular genetic trait. He campaigned vigorously for the active efforts to "breed the best in humanity into humanity and restrict the breeding of the worst."

Charles Davenport, a zoologist who was a disciple of Galton, established the very first genetics research center in America, in Cold Spring Harbor on Long Island, in 1905. It was called "Station For Experimental Evolution." This is where Davenport set up a Eugenics Record Office where statistics were kept on Americans. Also, via this office, individuals and society could be advised on "how best to breed."

Eugenicists have, in general, throughout their short-lived history, tended to have taken a rather bad rap. In some cases this has proven to have been more than justified. Adolph Hitler makes a perfect example of the application of genetics gone bad as someone who didn't care about or concern himself with the different cultural kinds of inheritance, and instead, was totally blind to everything in society except his own values and class prejudices.

The legacy of eugenics is even today still in some of the United States Immigration Laws, and have been since 1921, thanks to a group of doctors and lawyers who recommended "selective immigration by refusing immigrants below the determined standard of excellence." This approach allowed for "defective heredity and disease to be kept out." Also, the "elimination of defectives...by segregation and, in extreme cases, sterilization. In this way the number of insane, feeble-minded, epileptic, criminalistic, and paupers can be greatly reduced in a generation or two.''

Just imagine yourself finally disembarking after an uncomfortably long ocean voyage at the place that you've dreamed of for so many years, night after night in your oppressed little village in Poland—Ellis Island, the great portal to the "American Dream." Weary and frightened, with exhausted and cranky children in your arms, knowing only a handful of well-selected words in English, you are suddenly confronted with this new science of eugenics. What an overwhelming, terrifying and humiliating place Ellis Island must have been to many.

When it comes to eugenics, the major problem is (and has been since its conception) this—just who among us is qualified to give the ultimate definition on what is the "best" and what is the "worst" in the human race?

And finally, what, if anything, does all this talk of genetics have to do with obsessive-compulsive disorder? It really was not that very long ago (not even a full generation) that people with epilepsy, manic depression, or Tourette's Syndrome were looked upon as "nuts" because of their twitches, seizures, compulsions and variety of behavioral disturbances. Today, scientists know that these disorders have their basis in a biological malfunctioning. They now know for certain that these diseases are neurological disorders, not merely symptoms of "social disorganization." Scientists also now are finding that these biological imbalances are much more common than they had previously thought.

These types of neurological disorders are far worse than any other disease, because "they interfere with the functions of the Mind as well as the wholeness of the Body." That young man standing on the street corner in your hometown, shouting obscenities at the top of his lungs to people going by, all the while compulsively picking up scraps of paper off the sidewalk and shoving them into his trouser pockets, is a real, live, breathing example of this.

Genetic linkage has long been recognized as a powerful method for the elucidation of the influence of genetic factors in complex disorders. The DNA Committee report from Human Gene Mapping Workshop 10 (Kidd, et al., 1989) has compiled details of almost 2,000 polymorphic markers detectable with molecular DNA techniques. It is clear that several thousand markers exist and await detection. In the last decade or so it has become possible to construct a genetic map for humans with some of these markers (Helms, et al., 1988). Thus, genetic linkage methodology has become an increasingly important tool in the study of the inheritance of complex disorders such as Tourette's Syndrome and Obsessive-Compulsive Disorder (Pauls, et al., 1990).

Dr. David Pauls, from the Child Study Center and the Department of Human Genetics at Yale University, has focused his work almost exclusively on

Tourette's Syndrome and related disorders. As Dr. Pauls writes, "Although current diagnostic conventions exclude the diagnosis of OCD in individuals with TS, a significant percentage of patients with TS have prominent OC symptoms." Indeed, in his original 1885 description of the syndrome that today bears his name, Giles de la Tourette anecdotally reported an association between recurrent motor and phonic tics and obsessive-compulsive behaviors. Once again, as Dr. Pauls writes, "It has been suggested that the development of OC symptoms is part of the natural course of illness of patients with TS."

So, although the etiology of Obsessive-Compulsive Disorder remains unknown, several clinical investigations during the past 50 years have indicated that OCD is familial. To those of us who have this disease, this news is not a surprise. Once again, although the genetic basis of OCD is poorly understood, there is increasing evidence that the underlying etiological factors responsible for symptoms in at least some patients with OCD, TS and CMT (chronic multiple tics) are the same (Pitman, et al., 1987; Pauls, et al., 1986; Jenike, 1989). Therefore, there is a variety of evidence indicating that there may be an OCD spectrum of disorders that are genetically related, but for which the boundaries are as yet unclear (Black, et al., 1991).

Your human body is, in reality, one gigantic human genetic map—just waiting to be plotted—consisting of thousands of DNA markers. From the fiscal year of 1991, then president George Bush requested $156 million be committed specifically for the project of human gene mapping.

As Orwellian as it may sound, someday in the not too distant future, simple blood tests will be readily available to check on the healthiness of all our genes, before we can pass them along the family tree. It is obvious that, given time, it will be discovered that all of mankind's illnesses are nothing more than a long sequence of genetic events, all of them just waiting for their surreptitious codes to be broken.

"You couldn't deny that even if you tried with both hands."
"I don't deny things with my hands," Alice objected.
"Nobody said you did," said the Red Queen. *"I said you couldn't if you tried."*

Lewis Carroll

REALIZING THAT YOU HAVE OCD

I think that all small children like their little daily rituals. They can help to make this vast and sometimes overwhelming world they live in seem safer somehow. A particularly good example of this are bedtime rituals—the story, the tucking in, the last drink of water, and the good-night kiss. Most small children like these rituals carried out in a certain order every night, or it just doesn't feel "right" to them.

I don't think that my childhood bedtimes were very different than most other children's. For years now, I have racked my memory over and over again for anything I did as a child that, in retrospect, was somehow different or significant. I do remember liking to whirl in circles, as children are apt to do. However, I do have one strong recollection of that pastime—if I went, for example, five spins in one direction, then I had to be sure to go exactly the same number of spins in the opposite direction; otherwise I didn't feel "unwound." That is really all that I am able to recall from my early childhood about any possible hints to OCD in my future. But even now I'm not certain that it really was a hint. Perhaps it was simply child's play and nothing more.

Nonetheless, the dubious enjoyment of spinning in circles was left behind in my childhood, and aside from a fairly sporadic liking for neatness, the years between the 1950's and the 1980's seemed to be as everyday normal as they could be. Between 1978 and 1987 I had three children. After the birth of each son, I think perhaps I tended to become a bit more concerned with the state of cleanliness of my home, but I believe probably most of us are when we have babies starting to crawl everywhere. Anyway, I remember not feeling at all concerned about any of these small changes as I put them down to good "nesting" instincts. Also, the urge to have things a bit cleaner didn't interfere with any other part of my life at that time. In those days, housework to me was just something you did without giving it much thought. It was simply something to be gotten out of the way once, twice, or three times a week in order to fulfill part of your family obligations and then be able to go on to the more enjoyable things in your life.

Boy, are those days ever gone, at least for now. I'm not really clear on just exactly when everything started to change for me, it was so subtle. I think it was probably during my pregnancy with my third son. But, little by little, the need to keep certain spaces and objects spotless began to grow, slowly but steadily. Something that innocently started with my asking my family to "please leave your shoes by the door so as not to muddy up the carpet" and "please wash your hands" has in the past seven years turned into something that is totally frustrating and overwhelming to both myself and my family. These days my obsessive-compulsive disorder touches every aspect of our lives, at least to the extent of in the home. There are certain time-consuming rituals that must be done every single day of the week, before I am able to do anything else. Then, even after the daily rituals have been carried out, if I knock over a plant, spill some sugar, or make a mess in any other way, I must usually start the rituals all over again. Just simply wiping up the soiled spot isn't enough. You see, even though my eyes can see where, for example, the plant dirt is, my brain has lost the ability to believe my eyes. In other words, your brain is what allows you to "know" something is so. Your vision has absolutely nothing to do with it at all. So if I don't "know" for sure that I have cleaned up all the plant dirt, then it is just "safer" to clean everything all over again.

I'm not terribly certain what would happen if I didn't perform these rituals, but I'm pretty convinced that whatever the consequences are, they would probably include lightning bolts and severe pain. I have found that, at best, I am able to have a "Mexican stand-off" with these rituals. I can put off doing them for minutes, even sometimes for hours. But, nonetheless, eventually I will do them each day or the anxiety is unbearable.

For me the very cruelest result of having OCD is my inability these days to have anyone, no matter how close and well-loved they may be, come into my home. Certainly, without a doubt, the constant cleaning and the constant "Did you wash your hands?" is more than annoying to my family, but just possibly could be shrugged of as "Mom's a little weird" or "She's having her brain cramps again, just get out of her way." But how horribly painful it is to be literally terrified of having someone just "drop by to say hello." The panic is so great when this happens that I become physically ill. This reaction is such a primitive feeling—the need to keep others out in order to be "safe"—and my brain equates "clean" with "safe." I break out into a cold sweat when the paperboy knocks on the door.

What a truly amazing piece of work the human brain is! There seems to be absolutely no rhyme or reason to my daily rituals. There are only certain surfaces (floors—you really can eat off mine); countertops; stair bannisters; telephones; and some items, such as the remote control for the TV, that must be so clean that they squeak. Whereas I really don't seem to give a damn about that huge cobweb in the corner of the parlor; the inch of dust in the open kitchen cupboards, or the fact that all thirty-two of the windows in this house, not to mention the glass deck doors, desperately need a good washing inside and out. In other words, I'm so busy cleaning things on a daily basis that don't need it that it is impossible for me to find the time and energy to get to the things that do.

There is not a single move that I make in my house that I first don't ask myself, "Will this make something that I will have to clean up?" For years I have always done my own handy work in and around my homes. I have enjoyed doing the interior painting, wallpapering, stripping and refinishing of furniture, sewing for window treatments, etc. Right now, just the thought of doing any of these little projects would terrify me. These days, the list of things that I find that I am no longer able to do seems endless.

It took me a very long and painful time to find out that I was suffering from OCD. Off and on, over a period of two years, I went to counselors, therapists, pyschologists, and psychiatrists. I was given a different diagnosis with each new professional that I saw. Some of my favorites included being told that I was going through early menopause; a personal identity crisis; post-traumatic stress; and—my personal pick of all—hysterical and no doubt depressed, as I was a female type person..."take two valium and call me in the morning."

As the old J. Buffett song says,

"With all my running and all my cunning,
if we couldn't laugh, we would all go insane."

Apparently I hadn't laughed enough, because all of a sudden I was faced with what appeared to be a life of insanity stretched out before me. There really aren't any words I can use to accurately describe the emotions and the turmoil my family and I went through during this time of total uncertainty. Panic, fear, rage—none of these seem to capture the true essence of it all. It was a great deal like being left dangling over a steep precipice, tied to a thin, slightly worn rope.

Miraculously (and I don't use that word lightly), we just happened to stumble onto the answer to what was happening to me, by pure luck. One day my husband, by total chance, came upon some literature from the OCD Foundation. After skimming through the information, he excitedly brought it home to me. Isn't it strange how anything seems easier to deal with once you can put a name on it? From that day on, we have armed ourselves with every bit of knowledge printed about OCD to date. Imagine the weak-kneed relief of finding out that you are, after all, not going "Full-Goose-Bozo!" By educating myself about this disease, I am slowly losing much of my panic and anger. Although I am still frustrated with myself daily, I find that I am able to put this all into a healthier perspective, to forgive myself, and most importantly, to stop wallowing in guilt.

JESSE'S STORY

My name is Jesse; I'm thirteen and my Mom has OCD. She has had it for a few years now. When she was first diagnosed with it, it wasn't that bad just taking off our shoes before entering the house and taking showers every day, which we should have done anyway. Then, when we moved to a new house, we had to do very annoying things like washing our hands. With my Mom's OCD I can't have friends over and go inside to play Nintendo or watch TV. Right now my Mom's OCD is the worst it's ever been and I hope it's the worst it will ever be.

"WHY CAN'T YOU BE LIKE MIKE'S MOM?"

One day when my oldest son was almost thirteen, he looked me straight in the eye and said, "You embarrass me, Mom; I'm ashamed of you."

At that moment, as my heart started to break into thousands of tiny pieces, my husband jumped up from his chair, tossed down his book, and said, "Right! Okay, son, upstairs now! We'll pack her up and off and take care of this once and for all!"

Wide-eyed, Christopher said, "What do you mean?"

"Well," his dad said, "you're absolutely right! She does embarrass us; we are all ashamed of her, and we're tired of it all. What do you say we kick her out of here so we can all finally be happy?"

"But we can't let Mom go away!" exclaimed Christopher.

"Why not?" asked his dad.

"Because we love her!" said Christopher.

"In that case," replied Stephen, "instead of complaining and feeling sorry for ourselves, do you think we should find out all we can about obsessive-compulsive disorder, so we can learn to try to live with it?"

That day marked a turning point as to how my children and I started dealing with my disease. This is not to say that all the anger, frustration, and embarrassment that they were feeling magically disappeared. But somehow the boys' reactions to my OCD were finally able to be put into a better perspective. We were all beginning to be able to differentiate between Mom and Mom's Brain Cramps. As soon as we were able to make this separation, it seemed that our daily lives together began to take on a new dimension. Finally, my children and I were able to talk frankly about and discuss this disease that had intruded into our lives.

When something as devastating as OCD occurs in a family (most particularly to a parent), what would be the purpose of pretending it doesn't exist, that this horrible thing is not happening to us? Being only human, of course, I would like the people I love to think that I am perfect. But, the fact is, that I'm far from it, as are most of us. How could I possibly deny what this disease is doing to my family, especially to my children? How can I pretend that "nothing's changed" when it seems as if our entire world has been suddenly turned upside down? I can't—to try to do so would only be terribly harmful and very unhealthy to both myself and my family.

Unfortunately, I believe that most often children are very quick to blame themselves for any negative situation in a family. This type of reaction is common among young children who are experiencing a divorce or the death of a parent, for example. "Maybe if I'd just been a little bit better," the child will think to himself, "this wouldn't have happened!" As it is with most parents, the way that my sons perceive and ultimately feel about themselves during the course of their lives is at the very top of my priority list for them. How vital it is that they understand that none of these rituals are their fault or because of anything they do. When one of my children stands in front of me, as I'm cleaning away stuck in one place for the moment and says to me, "I think you've licked that spot now, Mom; believe me," it is so very important that he realize, when I'm not able to take his word for it, that it's not his Mom who doesn't trust and believe him, but his Mom's Brain. It's a difficult lesson for a child to learn that things can happen in this life that even Mom and Dad can't fix. Perhaps even more difficult than that is for them to understand and accept that when something horrible like OCD strikes a family, it's not always possible to find a place to put the blame.

Every single day, I make outrageous demands on my children in order to satisfy my rituals. The pain and guilt for what I'm putting them through is crushing. The good news is that they totally realize that not everyone in the world is like me, that this is not what most people would call the norm. It's so important that my youngest son especially, who never had a chance to know me before I became ill, know that "Mom does things a little differently than other people; everyone is very different and not everyone does everything the same way."

Overall, I think that my children are able to keep a fairly good perspective on my demands. I admit to taking their "emotional temperatures" frequently. We seem to have worked out a system that uses a lot of hugs, tears, jokes (actually some pretty sick ones), and often, yes, even the dreaded "A word"—anger. There is a hard and fast rule in this house that when they have simply had it with my Brain Cramps, anyone is free to look me in the eye and tell me just how pissed off all of this is making them at that particular moment. I in turn will usually agree, "You're right; it's a drag." Then we'll sort of shrug and someone will make a, usually tasteless, joke. This method may be rough, but it sure beats the alternative, which would be my family eating and consequently choking on their frustrations due to me.

Because of my disease, my obligations to my sons are perhaps a bit more than your average "normal" mother would have. For the moment, we all live with a fact—that being that I have OCD and, so far, we have not had any luck in stopping or reversing it. Because of this unpleasant fact, I feel that I now have two choices open to me.

A: I can go through each and every day feeling oh-so-sorry for myself and my family, and show my children how their mother rolls over when faced with adversity.

B: I can concentrate on the good things we all have together, such as mutual love, liking, and laughter, and I can show my boys that their mom doesn't fold in the face of a difficult situation. I can show them that we will work around it and make sure that we still have a good quality of life together, depsite this disease.

I pick "B."

CHRIS'S STORY

My name is Chris; I am Connie Foster's eldest son. I feel a little uncomfortable about talking about my Mom's disease, but I will try to tell about living my life with a person who has OCD.

At first, when this first started and I was old enough to understand, I really hated my Mom. I kept asking her why she just couldn't stop cleaning. She would try to explain over and over again why she couldn't, but I still did not understand. The only things that I understood was that she couldn't stop, no matter what, and that she had tried several types of medications to stop. She always said she loves me, and when she said that I would say to her, "If you really loved us, why can't you stop cleaning all the time so I can do stuff other kids get to do at home?" That was another drawback; I couldn't have friends over unless they stayed outside or in a laundry room we have connected to our house. I have a friend, Mike, who lived right across a field behind our house. We are best friends still, and we were best friends when we were kids. But the hardest thing to tell Mike, the first time he came over to my house, was that he could not come in. He asked why, and I tried to explain the situation but he didn't understand. But after three or four times of explaining, he understood somewhat. After that, he really didn't mind playing outside all the time.

Coming into the house is an operation that takes the cake. I thought that cleaning the house top to bottom every day was the stupidest thing in the world. I have to take my shoes off in the laundry room to cut down on the amount of dirt that enters the house.

I am now fourteen and I understand just about all there is to know about the kind of OCD that my Mom has. I don't hate her anymore, but I do get frustrated with her. If we are in a discussion about it she usually makes a joke about it. I have two friends in school who know about my Mom's OCD. They never mention it to me or anybody else, which is fine with me because I avoid talking about it with anybody.

It is very difficult for me to live with my mother, but I just tell myself that she is not to blame for having to clean all the time. By telling myself this, it makes it easier for me to talk with her without getting mad. All things considered, we are a loving family that communicates very well.

"Doesn't Mean That Much To Me
To Mean That Much To You"
"Harvest" by Neil Young

ON BEING DIFFERENT

We all have very different reactions to illnesses in not only ourselves but in others as well. Why is it that some illnesses seem just a touch more acceptable than others sometimes? If you mention to someone that you have, for example, cancer, they are generally shocked, upset, but still accepting and often even supportive of you and your disease. But mention to the same person that you have, say, schizophrenia or any other neurologically related disease, and watch them smile politely as they fade from your life forever. I do realize that this is a rather large and unkind generalization to make on mankind. But I have come up against this type of unthinking attitude more than once since developing obsessive-compulsive disorder, as I'm fairly certain that most of you who share this disease have.

However, what really bites is when I am confronted with a medical professional who has this narrow-minded way of thinking. Also having multiple sclerosis, I have spent what feels like a great deal of time in the medical community. One of only many, but certainly the biggest, determinations that I have made from all this exposure to physicians is that, apparently in order to feel that they are acting more professional, many doctors seem to treat you, the patient, as your disease rather than as the person that you are.

I remember when Anafranil became available in the States and I, of course, was very eager to try it. At that time all I had available to me was an internist in the small town that I live in. With a great deal of trepidation, while in his office one day, I told him that I had OCD and would he please write me a scrip for this new drug? I had really done my homework on this medication, even phoning the makers of the product, I was so excited to try it. But, sadly, it turned out that the instinct that I had about disclosing my OCD to my doctor was correct—right on target, in fact. His mouth dropped open for the longest time, and when he was finally able to close it, the very first words that he said to me were, "I don't know, you don't act crazy!" This was a situation that normally I would have found pretty hilarious, having a somewhat bizarre sense of humor. Who knows, maybe it still would have struck me funny if it were happening to the woman next door; however, this was happening to me, and I vividly remember the overpowering feelings of disgust (for his ignorance), rage, and humiliation that hit me at that moment. So, as I still had my pride left (at least a small amount), did I take a firm, moral stance on this subject, square off my shoulders, and patiently explain to him that "OCD" and "Crazy" are not necessarily synonymous conditions? No, I did not. Just like a good little girl, I sat politely smiling through it all. I even agreed with him, "No, I'm pretty sure that I'm not" (of course, the day was still early yet), the entire time holding my hand out, wanting what I hoped was a miracle prescription. Well, I got the prescription (which didn't, after all, turn out to be my miracle), but I lost the doctor. For every time that I had an appointment with him after that day of my "confession," he would always say, without fail, as I was leaving his office, "I don't know, Connie. I still don't think you're crazy." I learned two very valuable lessons from that experience. First of all, if I ever were going to "go crazy," those visits probably would have done it for me. So, I felt relatively safe on that score. Secondly, I learned that a medical professional can be just as biased and tunnel-visioned as the next fellow, especially if that particular disease doesn't happen to fall within their area of interest or expertise. So I guess what we are going to have to do here, is to drag these ignorant, insensitive people, even kicking and screaming, out of the Dark Ages, whether they want to be enlightened or not.

I strongly hold the theory that there is, without a doubt, something going on here based on socio-economics in the arena of brain chemical imbalances. Traditionally, anything having to do with the "personality" of the brain has been the sole subject area of psychiatrists, pyschologists, etc. This has been a mutually agreed upon, hands-off area for the "body" doctors. Very simply, you take your heart, knee, or hangnail problems to one, and your anxiety problems to the other. This system has seemed to work very nicely over the years for all doctors involved. But wait a minute! Hold the phone! Stop the presses! What if they've been totally wrong? Obsessive-compulsive disorder is a biochemical malfunctioning of the brain. The very word biochemical simply means "having to do with the chemistry of living matter." Therefore, call me dense, but I just can't seem to see how lying on a couch talking about whether or not you had a great childhood has anything at all to do with a physically caused illness. Is it possible that, due to lucrative business profits, somewhere, someone at sometime in the medical field could be intentionally withholding from their patients important and perhaps, in some cases, vital medical options and treatments?

"Psychiatry is the science of probing into a man's mind...in there it could be round or it could be flat...it's only an opinion."

Jimmy Stewart in "Anatomy of a Murder"

Obsessive-Compulsive Disorder is an odd illness in that there is no apparent physical stigma that can be seen on the body, something that can mark it as "ill" to the rest of society. OCD is, quite literally, in your mind. OCD is truly surrealistic. A disease that is often characterized by unusual and distorted thoughts and sometimes even images and motions. Obsessive-Compulsive Disorder is certain proof that everyone's sense of reality truly is an act of subjective reasoning. For example, what one may consider "more than clean" the man down the street may consider "not clean enough." But just what is it that shapes your reality? For each of us that evokes a different answer. OCD is really just another type of a disability. When I am out and about doing errands, for instance, my multiple sclerosis is an obvious disability to the people that I meet as I use a cane to help with balance and walking. My OCD, however, is not so obvious, especially if I'm not in my home. But believe me, that disease is far more a disability to me than my M.S. The disease of multiple sclerosis may prevent my body from always performing perfectly, but by far I find the OCD much more crippling. If by the mere wave of a fairy godmother's magic wand, I were to be given a choice between the two diseases, within a heartbeat I would choose to rid myself of the OCD forever and not mind one bit keeping the M.S. Having a disability is yet simply one more kind of the varieties of life—and life is certainly nothing if not full of variety.

Imagine what it feels like to have people, some of whom you have known for years and thought of as friends, turn away from you because you start to behave in a slightly different manner than they do. Like that doctor, their very first reaction is "crazy." Even after you have painstakingly explained the situation, the disease, the serotonin chemicals in great detail (not to mention the mere fact that only if you didn't know that the rituals you did every day were crazy would you be considered truly crazy). The painful truth is that if you happen to walk, talk and think in what is seemingly a slightly deviated fashion, then you could be considered a fairly suspicious individual.

Each and every society the entire world over has its very own set of standards that are considered to be acceptable. Sometimes these may be on a purely subconscious level, but these set standards are there—they do exist. These rules can and do serve many purposes. One of the main advantages is that they help to keep each member of their society comfortable with one another and safe. This way, they are all living with each other is such a way that is clearly understood among themselves.

Now granted, if you are a member of a Brazilian rainforest tribe, as opposed to being a member of a small fishing village on the coast of Maine, then each of your rules and standards for daily living will more than likely vary somewhat. But the bottom line remains that within each of these two societies the members tend to behave basically in the same way, that is, however is considered acceptable in their own community.

I wonder, just what does happen to you if your society is a tribe in the rainforest and you suddenly develop odd movements and twitches or become a checker? I wonder if the people that already know and love you remember that, these strange rituals aside, you are still the very same person that they have known and loved for some time. Do the members of this tribe rally around you and offer much needed comfort, understanding, laughter, hope, and strength? Could it be possible that they would even revere you because just perhaps in the rainforest tribes being different is considered very special indeed?

Or instead do the members of this tribe turn from you, shun you, close you out because they don't understand your disease and they cannot begin to comprehend why you do your rituals without being able to stop. Even when they say to you, "Just stop it! You're not trying hard enough or you could!" You and your disease are so confusing; they don't need this now! I wonder if they force you out of the community into the forest to fend for yourself, away from the rest of the society so that you will no longer shame them, embarrass them, make them feel uncomfortable, or, even worse, frighten them.

Anything that seems abstract and different that people either don't understand or aren't familiar with can sometimes be extremely threatening and terrifying to them, that is, unless they happen to have more than three brain cells to rub together and are interested in becoming better informed about whatever the subject may be.

I really do wonder how they handle Obsessive-Compulsive Disorder deep within the Brazilian rainforest. I already know how society handles it in a small village in Maine.

"I know heaven will be my eternal home, but I'm not homesick yet."

OCD AND SUICIDE

Most days I wake up willing and more than ready to fight this monster called OCD to the end—I figure that it's just a matter of which will give out first, me or my brain chemicals. But I would be less than honest if I didn't admit to having the odd day now and then when I'd like to "Hop a ship and skate across the ocean without a sound." When I am hit hard with an off day like that, the weight of it all seems so damn overwhelming—I mean, just how much repetition and self-loathing can any one human being take? Has there been a study done on this question? Winston Churchill called these his "black dog days." To me they are more like endless, tunnel days—the sameness of it all stretching on and on before me as far as I can see. Somehow, though, I always seem to make it (if not completely with total gracefulness) usually unscathed through these black days of mine. Afterwards, when this crisis has also passed, I can't help but wonder just what it is that we humans have in us that won't allow us to easily give up, even when all the odds seem stacked against us.

Granted, life is chock full of obstacles, and adjustments are always having to be made, it seems. But when you've been down so long that it looks up to me, just what, exactly, is the key that makes us push on and try so desperately to maintain through all adversity?

Of course, for all of us this question has a different answer. I look around me at people that I know and I see deep pride in some and outright stubbornness in others that makes them fight so hard against what seems like all odds. There are some people who are just plain too mean and downright ornery to give up. There is fear of the unknown: as painful as their lives may be at the moment, at least it is familiar to them.

When I examine myself for the answer to that question, I find that what works for me, what keeps me going, what gives me the strength to keep struggling, is probably a big combination of outright stubbornness and a great deal of love for my husband and children.

Let's be nakedly honest here. When this disease starts closing in around you, sometimes you cannot help but consider whatever options may still be left open to you, such as what I see as the Big Sleep. Some days I am so tired of trying to organize my life around my OCD that I'm really not sure if I have the energy to make it through the very next five minutes. When I have a day (or days) like that, I am so filled with pain and self-disgust because I don't have the control over my life that I once did, that I can't help but think that my family would be much better off without me.

Why, if I weren't here constantly having my Brain Cramps, they could all be just like the Cleaver household. Beaver would be running in and out of the kitchen noshing on June's still-warm-from-the-oven oatmeal with raisin cookies, dropping crumbs all over the newly waxed kitchen floor, while his mom smiled. Big brother Wally, with his oil-stained hands, would be sprawled out on the chintz covered sofa in the floral living room, yakking on the phone with a buddy. Having spent all morning in the back yard tinkering on his '56 Chevy convertible, his greasy, mud-caked boots would be casually propped up on the gleaming mahogany coffee table.

My God, how I want to be able to be just like June Cleaver (actually I'd pass on the frilly apron) for my family. Part of loving someone is to want the very best for them out of life. So if I truly and sincerely want the best for my husband and sons, how can I continue to stick around and make them so frustrated? How can I, on a daily basis, deprive my children of a normal childhood with all the messes that naturally come along with it? What a horribly self-centered person I must be to impose my disease onto the very people that I love, not just every once in a while, but every single day of the week without relief.

Really, though, just what alternative do I have except to hang onto plenty of good old-fashioned hope for what tomorrow may bring me? Just because today is Monday and I'm not "balanced" yet doesn't necessarily mean that it couldn't happen on Tuesday.

Which is potentially more damaging to a child: to have a parent who's ill and doesn't always function like the rest of the neighborhood moms or dads, or to have a parent who's given up on the prospect of life's ever changing for the better and wacked themselves? No matter how much I may bother my children and husband with my OCD, I am still convinced that my overall presence, guidance and love in their lives matters much more to them in the long run than the daily annoyances of my disease. The fact that I have a biological chemical imbalance is just not the total sum of who I am. Despite the feeling at times that this disease is so overpowering, it really is only a very small part of me as a person.

We all have to find our own reasons to want to live and enjoy life. I think that when all is said and done, we can't expect to find those reasons in other people but only deep within ourselves. Ultimately, each of us has to take the full responsibility for the quality of his or her own life.

"Fan her head!" the Red Queen anxiously interrupted. "She'll be feverish after so much thinking."

Lewis Carroll

"Canst thou not minister to a mind dises'd;
Pluck from the memory a rooted sorrow;
Raze out the written troubles of the brain?"

"Therein the patient...must minister to himself."

MacBeth
William Shakespeare

OCD AND LIFE

THIS IS REAL LIFE, THIS IS NOT A TEST...REPEAT...THIS IS NOT A TEST.

Obsessive-compulsive disorder is not a fatal condition, only a seemingly relentless one. I've been told, assured even, that with OCD also come periods of waxing and waning. Well, I'm sure ready for a little waning right about now, as I'm sure my family is.

But in the meantime, while waiting to wane, it's up to me to figure out a way to make it through my current life in as unflinching a manner as possible. Because I happen to have two disabilities, I can't just blindly plod along being willingly unresourceful. Even when in the best of health, I think that's a shameful way to be.

I guess that I am just one of those really disgusting people who can't seem to stay unhappy or depressed for any great length of time. You know, one of those truly sickening Pollyanna types who really does believe that worrying is only paying the rent in advance, so to speak. I don't know why I'm like this (I've been accused, wrongfully I think, of even being perky), but I just figure that it doesn't cost any more to laugh. Either I'm a very strong woman or I'm just not very bright and therefore too dumb to get upset for very long. I don't really know. Maybe it's a combination of the two. All that I know is that I adamantly refuse to go through my days feeling permeated by defeat. I cannot make my OCD go away, no matter how desperately I want it to. I have a need to be totally honest with myself about this disease. I can no longer hide from it and the reflections that my having OCD has on my family.

At one time, expecially after having found the OCD Clinic at Massachusetts General Hospital, I really had an abundance of hope—excitement, even—that I would be cured. As far as I was concerned, it was just a matter of time. Of course, back then, when I said time, I meant I could just possibly spare twenty minutes for this. After all, just how difficult a thing could this be to get "fixed" now that I had, after so long a search, finally found the right place and the right people?

These days I know that there's a hell of a lot more that is unknown about our brains and their biochemistry than is actually known. So much for my quick cure. I try to be a bit more realistic in that I have accepted the distinct possibility of having to adjust myself to this disease of OCD for many years to come, perhaps even for the rest of my life. On the other hand, at 8:26 tomorrow morning, I could get just that phone call from my doctor at Mass. General that I've been waiting for. It really does all come down to good old basic hope, doesn't it? As long as I have hope of a cure being found, I can use that as strength to get through another day.

But I don't want to just "get through" my days. I've always been fond of the phrase "frittering your life away." It's one of those wonderfully old-fashioned but oh-so-true sayings from your grandmother's time. Daily, I waste enough time on my relentless rituals, so much so that I'm certainly not going to waste the remainder of my time by refusing to enjoy and see all the marvelous people and things that are around me.

PERSONAL SURVIVAL TACTICS: Mozart; Beethoven (I may be doing my rituals nonstop, but, by God, I'm listening to some of the most beautiful and breathtaking music ever written); my husband's wry wit and humor; Patsy Cline (now there was a gutsy lady!); Vivaldi's "Four Seasons" (which has the ability to quickly put things into perspective for my by making me feel insignificant and unimportant); my children's faces; Mr. Rogers, who tells me, personally, via the television every weekday, that "I like you just the way you are"; and a five-minute daily temper tantrum allotment—when needed and when I am alone. This is either when I viciously slam the lid down on the washing machine a few satisfying times or look for one of the neighbor's cats to kick.

In the past few years, as my OCD became increasingly worse, I have had to plumb a few depths and really exercise my imagination to come up with any small thing that will give me enjoyment and happiness. With OCD, your mind needs as many breaks as it can get by focusing on something good, anything that just plain tickles you. It's rather like taking a very mini holiday, if only for a few minutes, just to be able to forget for a bit that you have this disease. When you are endlessly confronted by this thing called obsessive-compulsive disorder, it's altogether too tempting and far too easy to let yourself feel worthless and depressed.

I suppose that if I lived alone, I could be as weird, eccentric and depressed as I wanted to be. However, I do have my family to consider. I can, as far as they're concerned, go ahead and be as weird and eccentric as I want, but they do mind if I'm depressed for more than ten minutes—unfair or not, this is just the way it is and it only serves to drag the rest of my family down. It's almost like I'm the "barometer" in this house, and if I'm "up" then the rest of the household is "up," too. I figure that I give my family more than enough confusion and trouble, I'm not going to add depression to the list.

The day that I stopped hiding and was honest with friends and family about my disease was the day that I took a big leap of faith in facing either the potential understanding or rejection from these people. It has turned out that there were a few who couldn't accept me the way I'd become, but, the initial hurt aside, it's still much easier to breathe now that I'm no longer hiding.

"Honesty is certainly not possible without courage. For unless a man has that virtue he has no security for preserving any other."
                                                                    Samuel Johnson

It was extremely difficult and painful to try to explain this disease to parents, brothers and sisters of both my husband and myself. (Actually, there still are some who don't know—surprise.) My main concern was, and still is, that they not be hurt or feel unwanted by the way that I am. OCD can be a pretty tough concept to grasp, but because they are family and they do love us, the general consensus seems to be, "We don't really understand this disease, but as long as your little family is happy together, that's what matters." Who could possibly ask for more than that?

From the time that I was very young, I have been lucky enough to have possessed a fairly good sense of self (or I suppose that you could call it arrogance). Of course we all want to be approved of and liked by others; that's part of being human. But, basically, I have always felt that as long as I knew and was sure of what I was doing, that it really didn't matter a great deal what other people thought. If anything, I'm only concerned with not what is thought of me but of any possible hurt that someone might feel because I can't entertain them in my home. At the moment, we return every dinner invitation by taking our hosts out to a restaurant, although lately I have come to realize that my inability to have them in bothers me a great deal more than it does my friends. They can't take this lack of hospitality personally, as they realize that it is my OCD that's holding me back. So now the thing that I worry about most is just how am I going to show the world what great taste in decorating I have if I can't let it through the front door?

How incredibly fortunate I am to know some very loving and supportive women. You men don't fully realize this, but we women are very good at nurturing each other when it's needed. Some of these women actually have OCD themselves, so needless to say, we completely understand one another even though we all have very different compulsions. One of my close friends grew up while her mother had OCD (and still does). So not only do I appreciate this woman for her kindness and wicked sense of fun, but she is the one I will talk to when I need a little help in putting my sons in the proper perspective with all of this. There are some people whom my husband and I have told who, although they don't really have a clue, have been very non-judging in their reactions. A wonderful example of this is that recently we re-financed our home. A problem quickly arose during this process when the bank we were dealing with wanted an appraiser to go through our house. As it was impossible for me to have anyone walking through here, my husband, in his usual straightforward and sensible manner, explained my situation to the bank. They, in turn, very nicely settled for accepting a video of our home that my husband shot just for them. Now I am willing to bet a substantial sum of money on the fact that neither the banker nor the appraiser are too up to date on OCD, but the point is that they were incredibly reasonable about it all.

I am always concerned about my sons' friends and just how they construe not being invited inside to play. Living as we do in a big, old, rambling New England-style house, we are fortunate to have a barn and outbuildings where things can be set up a bit in order for my boys to entertain their friends, at least under a roof, if they want. Not too long ago, my Jesse had two friends over, one of whom, being a new friend, had never been here before. The boy had apparently asked about going upstairs to see Jesse's room, and my son was patiently trying to explain the ins and outs of my OCD to him. First time visitors can be awfully tricky for my children! Anyway, this boy was having a pretty rough time understanding all that Jesse was telling him, and kept asking questions. Finally, Jesse's other friend, who's here frequently, becoming totally exasperated, took it upon himself to say, "Look, she just likes things cleaner than most other people do, but she's still nice!" Thank you, Alonzo.

I believe that one of the best gifts that can be given to my children is for them to be able to visit other people's homes. It's important that my boys be able to take the occasional holiday from my Brain Cramps and be reminded of just how the "other half" lives. We are so lucky to have extended family members who are always eager to have all three boys visit. In their grandparents' homes they are free to do the normal things that boys do, such as totally devastating a kitchen by "building" their own lunches. It's a refresher memory course on the knowledge that not all homes are run like ours. They need to be reminded that there is an end in sight for them, even if I'm not cured, and that they won't live surrounded by my rituals forever.

Yup, I guess it really is just easier for me to laugh rather than to cry; be up rather than down; be happy rather than sad. Whatever else may or may not be in my brain chemicals, gloom and doom aren't.

"He had given them (his friends) the most precious of gifts one can give another, and that is hope. With all the odds against him, he had proved that it was possible to get through this strange adventure of life, and to do it in such a way that is a tribute to human nature."

Samuel Johnson
by Walter Jackson Bates

STEPHEN'S STORY

What is it like to live with a loved one who suffers from OCD? From my perspective, it depends upon how one approaches life in general. That is to say, if you endeavor to deal with all the day to day problems life has in store for you in a forthright and direct manner, you can look at OCD as just another obstacle to be dealt with in your pursuit of a happy, productive relationship.

In my opinion, without a solid foundation of love and caring, any relationship is susceptible to failure. Living with a partner who is OC will definitely test to the limit the strength of that foundation. Your emotions will run the full spectrum of love, sympathy, anger and frustration, but all of these emotions will be put in proper perspective when you pause to reflect on the inner soul of your partner. When you feel in your heart the hurt and anger which radiates from the one you love because she is putting her loved ones through the same hell she is suffering, all of these emotions will sort themselves out.

The hardest thing for me to deal with, perhaps surprisingly, is not the inconvenience the children and I must endure in order to keep our family unit intact, but rather the wasted talent and energy which my wife has been blessed with. Because of her OCD she is precluded from exercising and exhibiting her vast array of talents and vibrant energy in any rewarding fashion. She is held back from being all that she can be as a mother and wife and friend because her rituals always come first. She is extremely entertaining and extroverted in any social setting, but can't entertain at home, which makes it difficult to maintain social relationships when you can't reciprocate with invitations to dinner.

It breaks my heart to watch her angrily scrub the floor for hours, hating herself every minute but powerless to do anything about it. It hurts to know that she thinks less of herself than she does of her friends and other children's mothers, who maintain "normal" households.

I know what she is, I know the stuff she's made of, I know the hardships she's endured, I know what she has made of herself, I know the values she holds, I know the values she instills in our children. I know what she doesn't know: that she is "more" than any of her friends and family will ever understand. It's painful to know all of this and watch her endure the feelings of shame and guilt she is powerless to control.

Do I resent having to live like this? Of course I do! Do I resent my wife because of this? Never! I know that no matter how much I dislike this, it pales in comparison to how she feels. She has to bear the burden of being responsible for the way we live. I wish I could share the burden with her, but I am powerless to do so. Perhaps for those of you with OCD, bearing this burden alone is your way of atoning to your loved ones. But perhaps it would be easier on those of us who love you if you would stop beating yourself up over it. When you feel bad, we feel bad.

My wife also suffers with M.S., which is a terrible disease, potentially crippling. However, I must state unequivocally that but for the OCD, the M.S. would be a walk in the park for my wife. OCD is a disease whose symptoms cannot be escaped or avoided by anyone in the family. We are all affected by it. M.S., on the other hand, limits its impact to the individual afflicted.

Some of you will undoubtedly ask the question that I have asked myself over the years—why put up with it? Why put yourself and your children through this? Why not end the relationship for your own peace and enjoyment and for the well-being of the children?

In my case there are various reasons: love; a sense of commitment; family; faith in God; and a deep-seated conviction not to run from adversity. I firmly believe that our children can be better men because of this. And last but not least, if you can still ask "Is it worth it?", then YOU JUST DON'T GET IT!

"WHAT'S WRONG WITH ME?????"

My name is Johnny and I live alone—in hell! Oh, sure, I have a family and sometimes a job. Sometimes I manage to go to school or get regular things done—like get up, get dressed, brush my teeth, eat a meal and be on my way. In fact, some days I'm such a good pretender that I can convince everyone that I'm "normal," but deep down, I know I'm not. Sometimes the frantic "crazy" side of me just won't leave me alone long enough to do anything "normal." I don't know what it is! Sometimes I think that I'm possessed or that maybe there are two brains in my head. All I know is that I think and do all these weird, bizarre and "crazy" things, and that sometimes, no matter what, I just can't stop. Over and over and over, the same thoughts, the same behaviors. It's like my brain never gets the message that I already did it once. It's done and I know it is, but I just have to keep going—I can't quit. But of course, I keep all this inside. In fact I don't dare tell anyone because they may lock me up. I just have to keep lying and making up stupid excuses why I do all these "crazy" things. But today I think I'm going to burst; my head is just going to explode if I don't tell someone about all this. I'm so tired. I'm sick and tired of being sick and tired. If I can't find help I just want to die—not suicide, I just want to lay down and die. So I guess I'll just be brave and tell you all about me, and if you lock me up it couldn't be any worse than what it's like now. So here goes—here is my list of all my crazy thoughts and behaviors:

Wearing the same clothes, over and over, even though it is really embarrassing.

I keep all the paper sacks and boxes that my clothes come in. One day my mom took six full garbage bags of sacks and boxes out of my closet. I was so ashamed.

Letting my hair and fingernails get really long because I can't cut them, or sometimes I have to cut them really short so I feel clean and I do it every other day until my fingers bleed. I can't write or say certain words, even words like "table" or "chair" that are usually no big deal.

Sometimes I try to get a friend to do weird things with me, like jump back and forth over gutters or cracks in the sidewalk.

Sometimes I have to jump around like a monkey and make certain faces. I make strange noises and then maybe I just have to stare at a certain spot on the wall, sometimes for hours.

When I drive down the street I always think that I ran over somebody and I have to drive around the block and check for a body in the road. I've driven around the block ten or twenty times trying to convince myself that I didn't hit anyone. Then when I get home I feel compelled to call the police and confess that

I've hit someone, but they always tell me that no one has been hit in that location that they know about.

Sometimes I can't touch other people; my brain tells me that they are contaminated and if I touch them I will be, too. And then sometimes I have to touch people—in certain places on their backs and exactly twelve times.

I count everything—everything—over and over, except odd numbers. I can't say or think odd numbers or something bad will happen to someone I love. I have to count how many steps to my bedroom and usually when I get to the top I think I counted wrong so I have to go to the bottom and start over. Sometimes I don't get to bed until three or four in the morning because I'm going up and down the stairs counting steps. I'm always afraid I'm going to stab someone or poke a lit cigarette in their eye. Then I have to wash my hands so the thoughts will go away.

When I talk to people sometimes I have to repeat everything they say to me. It really drives them crazy. I try to just mumble it but usually I say it out loud. I have to make lists—lists of lists of lists. Things I'm supposed to do and things I want to do and things I never could do; but day after day I make lists of these things.

I'm scared to death of germs!!! I just know they are everywhere. I can't drink out of a drinking fountain, or touch my clothes after I take them off. Sometimes I put my clothes through the wash five or six times in a row just until I get the "right feeling" that the germs are gone. Then I have to wear gloves to put them in drawers and even then they might touch something else with germs on it and I'll have to start all over again.

I'm afraid of getting AIDS, even though I know I haven't had sexual contact with anyone who has AIDS and even though I haven't had anyone bleed on me and I don't do IV drugs.

Sometimes I have to take three or four showers in a row and wash with Listerine and Clorox before I feel clean and safe.

I have to clean my kitchen until it is just perfect. I scrub the sink over and over and then I put on rubber gloves and pour rubbing alcohol on the counters to be sure they are clean.

I use roll after roll of paper towels to wipe my hands after I wash. I might throw away half a roll until I get to the right towel that "just feels OK" to use.

I can't go to the bathroom in a public place—not ever, no matter what. Sometimes I can't even sit on my own toilet seat until I've cleaned it and sterilized it with alcohol.

I can't throw certain things out. I have bags full of paper scraps with things I've written. I'm afraid that if I throw them out I will toss something really important and then won't be able to get it back. I have to turn the lights in my room on and off and on and off—sometimes for hours or until the bulb goes out. Then when I finally get it out so that it "feels OK" I have to leave through the door in just the right way. I usually mess it up and have to jump back and forth across the threshold dozens of times.

I've ruined my car key and car door lock by locking and unlocking the door over and over. Sometimes I might be outside three hours making sure the door is really locked and that it is locked just right!

I can't read the obituaries in the newspapers. If I even look at them I have to go wash my hands right away or I'm afraid I will die, too.

When I watch TV, I can't look at certain things, like people with diseases or I just know it will be transmitted to me.

I can't see or touch anyone with a cold sore (herpes) on their face or I will get one, too. Sometimes I have to go the emergency room at the hospital to have a doctor check my lips for cold sores.

I have obsessions that my best friend is adopted and that we were actually brothers even though I know I wasn't adopted and that we are only three months apart in age.

I have a compulsion to eat things off trees or plants and then I get another obsession that what I ate was poison and I go make myself vomit.

I'm afraid that someone will kill my parents while I'm asleep and they will blame me. Then I get afraid that maybe I will kill them while I'm asleep and not know that I really did it.

I feel like such a failure! I don't know why I'm just not strong enough to stand up to this monster. Why can't I "just say no"? I have no feeling of self-worth or self-esteem and I'm sure God must hate me or why else would he give me this? Maybe I'm just a bad person and I did something horrible to deserve all this. I wish I was crazy enough not to know this is all crazy. I feel lost, hopeless and totally helpless. WHAT'S WRONG WITH ME???

The preceding tells the heart-wrenching pain that is Johnny's life; but actually, Johnny is not "a" person. These thoughts, obsessions, behaviors, compulsions and fears are direct quotes collected from statements of self-disclosure by past and present members of our support group. For many of us, we never knew that anyone, besides ourselves, had any of these bizarre things going on in their lives. All we knew was that we were not "normal." What an incredible feeling of relief we experienced when we realized we were not alone. For once in our lives we found that we could talk about and share those things which we had held as our darkest secrets. What an experience to be loved unconditionally by a group of people who share the same pain. How many years did we go on thinking that there was never to be an escape from our own private hell, and then all of a sudden to find the key to the door, a safe place where we could explore our "dark side" and begin a new life. We found out that we had a disease called Obsessive-Compulsive Disorder or OCD. We found out that this is caused by a chemical imbalance in our brains, not by demons or worse, by God, who wanted to punish us because we were so evil. We found out there was medicine, behavior therapy, and support from others who had gone before us. We found out that this disease happens to a lot of people (perhaps as many as one in seven), and that it has been passed down genetically throughout history. We even found out that some very well-noted and famous people had OCD. Most importantly we found hope! If you identify with any of the things shared in this article, then know that there is help. We encourage those who have gone before us to come back and share your experience, strength and hope with new-comers, and we beg of you—if you are still out there, alone, and in OCD prison, come get a key to begin your journey of healing. Join our group and find hope! We need you as much as you need us.

OCD Support Group
Salt Lake City, Utah
For more information, please phone 801-583-2500 and ask for Suze.

JUDY'S STORY

Before October 19,1990, no one in my family had ever heard of Obsessive-Compulsive Disorder. As our oldest son returned to college for his senior year, something seemed different about him. We attributed it to the tensions of planning a future, be it looking for a job or going on to graduate school. His telephone calls sounded strained and consisted of complaints about his roommates constantly interrupting his thoughts. Knowing things were not quite right, I telephoned our pediatrician who agreed to see him when he came home for a fall break. He agreed to check his health and also to do a drug screening to be sure he was not on drugs. I agreed, though in my heart, I knew this son of mine, an Eagle Scout, high honor student, a health conscious athlete and a church goer, was not involved in drugs. Upon checking my son, the pediatrician found him depressed and referred us to a pyschiatrist. After two visits, it was this psychiatrist who made the initial diagnosis of OCD and began prescribing Anafranil.

Life was never the same. The symptoms of the illness became intensified, and the Anafranil with all its side effects was not effective. Returning to school after fall break was not possible because our son became so afflicted by the routine of counting that he became dysfunctional and completely incapacitated.

Our family life centered around our son. He needed help to get out of bed, dress, eat, come out of a room, close the compactor, shut the refrigerator, get up from a chair, and the most difficult aspect of the illness was watching him pull his hair out to count the strands. Counting comprised his entire existence. Until he had a certain "feeling" that the counting had gone "right," he could not move on. Driving became impossible as he always felt he had run over someone and would return to the "spot" over and over. He would sit behind the wheel for as long as four hours counting until he had the series of numbers correct in his mind. Staring into the rear view mirror became an issue and driving became a hazard. He lost interest in his appearance and avoided the bathroom because he became "stuck" in particular rooms and found that the room captured him as he frantically counted to get the right feeling. Screams of frustration, along with vulgarities, echoed through the rooms of the home that had been such a happy place before all this began.

It took some time for my husband and I to go through the denial stage and begin to pull ourselves together and decide what to do next. We began by reading all we could about the illness. There was some comfort in knowing others had also experienced this bizarre and little-known illness. We joined a support group where we were fortunate to meet and become friends with Patricia Perkins, the founder of the OC Foundation. She recommended many doctors, some at Massachusetts General in Boston and the Neuroscience Department at Yale. We visited both places and learned all we could. Our son became an outpatient at Yale and participated in a study of OCD patients and the experimental drug Fluvoxamine. It was a double blind study with only the pharmacist knowing if the patient was receiving the real medicine or a placebo. At the end of the sixteen week study, there was no change in symptoms. Yale now began to experiment with Fluvoxamine and other medications. In October, 1991, a combination of drugs began to make a difference. Within one week, we began to see an improvement. After twelve months of anguish for all of us, we began to have hope that life would return to normalcy for our son and for our other three children and ourselves.

How painful it was for a mother to watch her son suffer and not be able to do anything to help. Many nights I stayed up all night with him, sleeping on the sofa and hoping he would fall asleep and not be entangled in the counting routine. How often I thought of the days when I could make everything O.K., and here I was unable to help with an illness I found so hard to understand. Counseling was helpful. It helped me to understand that it was not my fault. A chemical imbalance, it is felt, is the underlying cause. Yale asked my husband and me to participate in a parents' study of OCD children. We agreed and participated in a year-long study. We agreed to be videotaped and hoped to be of help to other families.

October, 1993, will be three years since the ordeal began for my family. Our son is on the road to recovery. Along with the medications from Yale, he sees a behavior therapist once a week. This has made a remarkable impact on his behavior. I firmly believe it is the combination of medication and behavior therapy that is the most effective way to deal with this illness.

Family life has become more normal. Our second son, a senior in college, is applying to medical school and would like to do brain research and major in neuroscience. Our third son, also in college, is studying pre-medicine. Our daughter, also in college, is studying nursing. The strain of the past three years is fading and there is more laughter. Love was always present, though at times patience ran thin. A supportive family is the key to helping the OCD patient. It took time for my other children to understand this illness. What took the most time was the understanding that he could not help his behavior and could not control the actions. My husband and I spent hours counseling our other children. What if it were cancer? Would we give up on him? This illness is like a cancer of the brain. It destroys the life of the afflicted, making him an individual constantly hiding his behavior.

My life will never be the same. I realize how vulnerable we are. The "ideal" family that I perceived us to be had traveled to hell and back. I still fear that things will again become unraveled and there will be a setback. My son has returned to college part time and hopes to finish his college degree next summer. The illness has robbed him of three years of his life and has aged me both physically and mentally. I am now trying to be a support for other mothers in similar situations. Being a teacher, I have become an advocate for children with OCD. I continue to read all I can, attend lectures at the nearby Institute of Living, counsel parents and lend a listening ear. I do understand what they are feeling and the heartache they are suffering. I have suffered, but nothing can compare to the suffering my son endured for three years. He will never be one hundred per cent cured, but all we hope for is a happy life that enables him to live a near normal life.

Judy
Farmington, Conn.

BETTY'S STORY

I had never heard of OCD before the spring of 1987, when I learned that my son was suffering from this condition. After that, I began to look at some of my own thoughts and reactions. Had I been a victim of OCD myself? Now that the medical profession had come up with a name and was looking into possible causes and cures, I wondered.

During the past, I must have simply believed that everyone with an active mind would probably think bizarre thoughts from time to time, and that no one with any imagination would be completely immune to intrusive thoughts and, at times, the most extreme exaggerations of fantasy. Obsessive-Compulsive Disorder is a most disabling condition that has crippled the lives of countless individuals the world over. It surprised me that it was diagnosable and that it could be treated and often controlled by medication. In seeking an answer for my son, I discovered my own basic problem.

OCD sufferers are affected in various ways. Many of these individuals seem to be highly sensitive and to have a tendency to be perfectionists; and some are determined to have things done their own way always—regardless. I used to have a difficult time making beds. I had to get out every wrinkle. I had a difficult time leaving little sores on my face alone. I wanted to get off every little imperfection. I had a strong urge to check the range in the kitchen, the windows, the furnace, the lights, the water.

My father used to say I had a "one-track" mind. I like to follow through and get things done; but isn't that good? If I know what I want, and it has a good and acceptable purpose and I am willing to stay with it until it is done, and when a person finds a subject fascinating and dwells on it to the exclusion of other things, is it fair to call this inner urge a "disorder"? I have heard that my father himself used to concentrate on his studies to the exclusion of all else, no matter how much noise those around him might make.

I found my response to things often involved my religious education, which seemed too often to contradict what I held as truth. I blame what happened to me largely on a strict disciplinary background, a tendency on the part of a number of my close relatives to be superstitious, and my family's concept of God. This concept, grounded in the Christian tradition, rested on blind faith rather than on known truths. The church's teachings often frightened me, and I must have built up a fear that some superstitious nonsense may come to mind and make matters worse.

I would at times retrace my steps, an idiosyncrasy I did not understand then. Sometimes I would pause before going through doorways. I finally attributed these things to a feeling of insecurity that kept my nerves on edge. In trying to unravel the mystery, I looked back into my childhood relationships with my parents and their parents. I tried to analyze why I responded to certain things in certain ways. This searching for answers brought to light important truths for me. I was eaten up with fear and superstition, and a religion that held me in logical contradictions that forced me into uncertainty as to what I believed and what I was expected to believe, and this kept me in a mental tug-of-war.

I was overwhelmed by the greatness of the God who rules our lives and knows everything that has ever happened from the beginning of time to the present second and everything that is going on at this moment in everyone's mind, and everything that will go on infinitely into the infinite future! I had been overcome with not simply awe, but a fear that I would not always please this all-powerful, omnipresent Being. I must have often been frightened over what I believed to be a strict, disciplinary, unbending Master, who was overseeing everything in my life down to the minutest detail, a being I was told loved me, yet was at the same time ready to make me suffer if I should step out of line in the slightest degree. Often I felt uncomfortable, as though I had done something wrong, but what? I really did not know. Had religion and fear been so ingrained together within me that my nerves simply could not tolerate the tension?

I had long ago slipped into uncomfortable habits, yet not to follow their pattern could cause discomfort, too. A terror I could not explain could paralyze me with fear. Sometimes I would have to wait for just the right thought to come; and the more my thoughts disturbed me, the more I seemed to think them, at times. They could hold me in a firm grip. They became obstacles to many of the things in life I had hoped would become realities. I had boxed myself into all sorts of illusions. I was afraid of God's wrath (but for what I do not know). I was uncertain and afraid of my chance thoughts, and I sometimes tempted myself by breaking, or not breaking, my own made-up rules. Chance seemed to control me.

When going through doorways, I would often stop short and sift through my thoughts to be sure that in passing from one room to another, I would think only good things. A threshold became a threat. If I found I could not stand there and wait, but had to go through that doorway, I could force myself to do this, but the trauma could be awful. But the fact that I could go through it and my life went on as usual surely taught me something. Eleanor Roosevelt is credited with this: "I believe that anyone can conquer fear by doing the things he fears to do, provided he keeps doing them until he gets a record of successful experiences behind him." And this: "You gain strength, courage and confidence by every experience in which you really stop to look fear in the face. You are able to say to yourself, 'I lived through this horror. I can take the next thing that comes along.' You must do the thing you think you cannot do.''

Fear could drive me to retracing my steps. This seemed to ease the tension I felt, but it took a long time for me to understand why I felt obliged to do this. I remember driving around the block numerous times. If anyone had asked why I was doing this, I would have to think up a plausible explanation that would not embarrass each of us. I wouldn't have wanted anyone to know that my desires to do everything just right and my terror if I did not have only Godly thoughts could be driving me crazy, and I secretly hoped that no one ever noticed what I was doing when I found an uncomfortable urge to repeat my actions.

Sometimes unwanted thoughts could suddenly come from nowhere, and instead of brushing them off as unimportant (as I would do now), I would try the only thing I could imagine to help at the time to satisfy my longing for the peace I sought, and I suppose that by retracing my steps I hoped that I could erase the wrong thoughts and replace them with right ones. It was like a child's game, but no one knew this but me. When the urge to retrace my steps was too strong, I sometimes go "round and round until it felt right." God seemed to be in some abstract way watching me constantly, and it made me nervous. I never wanted to allow the flaws I found in whatever I did to be the final product of my work (whatever it was), and I would try and try again until I could satisfy myself, I suppose, that I had done everything to the very best of my ability. And so, round and round the block I would go, or in and out of doors, or write and erase and write again. Could this be what is still happening to my son and to other conscientious, God-fearing sufferers of OCD? My son had once confessed to me that he had "wrong thoughts." (This was before I realized that I did, too. As I said before, I thought everyone with an active mind probably had fantastic thoughts from time to time.)

Is anyone born with the unnatural responses of OCD? I am confident that all my babyhood (if I am correct) was nothing more than an accumulation of thoughts and habits that were added to my basic baby nature. If the fault lay in my thinking process and my conditioned response to my thinking, then my thoughts, and these alone, were the culprits.

Obsession does not necessarily mean a "disorder." It is only so when out of control. No one would say that Shakespeare or Leonardo da Vinci had a "disorder" when driven to complete their masterpieces, or that the builders of bridges and skyscrapers, inventors and world explorers necessarily have a "disorder." But when obsessions are driven and misdirected by superstitious fears and unwanted thoughts, these things can force a person to spend time in rituals that are loathsome to the individual, and definitely "disorders."

Obsessions can put meaning into life and raise expectations toward worth-while goals. The compulsions that follow obssesions can give a necessary drive to accomplish our meaningful goals. I have been obsessed with writing this paper, and my drive to keep at it has made its finished product possible. There has been no "disorder" involved, only a strong wish (obsession) and will (compulsion) to express myself in a way that may help others, who are still searching for a way out. Life can be beautiful, and positive in every sense of the word.

Betty P.
Charleston, S.C.

MICHAEL A'S STORY

June 1988

I had to touch everything in my room a specified number of times. This number was now a 3 with 9 being a perfect multiple (3 x 3) and 9 x 3 equaling 27, I had to touch everything 27 times. Often I had to touch everything 30 times. Only because 30 was a 3 with a 0 at the end of it. Then I did the same thing with both my doors. All together it took about 20 minutes. Twenty minutes of my life were wasted playing with the door and various items in my room. 20 MINUTES! I could have watched 40 commercials in that time. I could have listened to side 1 or side 2 of "Destroyer" by KISS. I could have gone outside and run up and down the street. I wasted 20 minutes of my life on compulsions.

I had a bit of trouble entering my aunt's house. I had to enter with my feet going steadily in a certain pattern. When I got home that night I related everything that had happened to me that day. My mother didn't make that much of these things at that time. I think that it confused my mother more than anything else. She had never heard of anything like this before. I went to sleep that night feeling lonely, empty, and confused. This thing was beginning to scare me.

July 1988

Things became worse around the house for me and my family, who still had no idea of what I was going through. My mother consulted a pyschologist who was a nice guy, but really wasn't trained in this area. He knew a little about OCD (or so he said), but he didn't have the slightest idea of how it was affecting me. I started to hate trying to talk with him and he didn't understand what I was telling him anyway. He referred us to a psychiatrist who probably got his degree out of a Cracker Jack box.

August 1988

We went to see this fool my psychologist had referred us to. The man knew nothing about OCD in children and didn't know how to treat me. His only other OCD patient was a man in his twenties. The man was an incompetent in a medical uniform. How he managed to become a doctor, I have no idea. He put me on a level of medication that was much too high for my size, age and body weight. And he strung us along for weeks until my mother diagnosed me as having OCD. She had read about it in the August issue of "Good Housekeeping." We then stopped seeing this fool and searched for better help. At the beginning of September I started my second year of junior high school. Unfortunately, things had snowballed with the OCD, but the junior high staff was very supportive. They wanted to learn more about this disorder. They put me in some private classes and tried to keep school about as enjoyable as possible for me.

October 1988

My grades are getting worse and my life is beginning to become completely consumed by compulsions.

November 1988

I heard about this miracle drug called Clomipramine on a talk show and we looked into getting it.

December 1988

It was Christmas time and my emotions were all screwed up. My sister, who introduced me to Ozzy and Motley Crue, was coming up with her husband. He was the closest thing I'd ever get to having a big brother. And yet, my OCD was starting to get out of control, even though I was on Prozac which was supposed to help me deal with the OCD. The Fool had prescribed this.

January 1989

It was a new year but I'm still battling with an old problem. I was sleeping on the floor at night with all my clothes on, sneakers and all. Things were becoming a bit scary for me and my parents. I was afraid I was going to die if I didn't play with the TV dial. I thought my mother would die if I didn't touch the doors coming into my house. My sister was pregnant with her first child and I had to do a wide variety of rituals in the bathroom—touching the sink, the mirrors, the back of the toilet, along with all the magazines and basic bathroom literature lying around, to insure that she would not have a miscarriage. My neurologist referred us to the OCD Clinic at Mass. General.

February 1989

I went to the clinic where I had a long meeting with a doctor and a man who I believe was a med student. They asked me basic questions just to make sure that I wasn't schizophrenic. It was quite boring and strangely enough, that was the last that I saw of that doctor. She referred me to Dr. Biederman, who was the only one authorized to give me the medication that we thought would solve this whole thing.

April 1989

I had my first session with Dr. Biederman, who was cool for a doctor. Unfortunately, he couln't prescribe Anafranil for me as I am an epileptic and the side effects of that drug could put me into a coma, or worse yet, kill me. He changed my Prozac dosage and set me up with an appointment with my behavior therapist, Dr. Minichielo. He was to help me a lot in the months to come.

May 1989

My aunt had a serious car accident on the way to my sister's baby shower. I blamed myself. I figured that if I had done the compulsions this thing wouldn't have happened. Dr. M. tried to talk me out of this but I still wasn't sure.

June 1989

My aunt was recovering and I was beginning to realize that the car accident wasn't my fault, and that I could stop doing compulsions if I tried. I'd graduated from junior high with a D- average. I should have stayed back, but instead I got a tutor over the summer to move on to high school.

July 1989

I hate this tutor. All she seems to care about are disgusting insects.

August 1989

I hate this tutor. Get me out of this nauseating situation.

September 1989

I started high school this month. I had a lot of trouble with my compulsions and most of the staff did not believe that OCD actually existed. They thought that it was just an excuse for laziness. It's sad to think that there is so much ignorance surrounding us. My first guidance counselor and math teacher/dictator of discipline did not believe any of this. My first guidance counselor was replaced and my math teacher was also replaced. We contacted a few doctors in Boston and they shot down a few people at Abington High. Basically, I was harrassed no more except by the dictator of discipline.

October 1989

I was doing terribly in my classes and there was really nothing I could do about it. For instance, I was taking modified algebra and I couldn't understand any of it. My neurologist later explained that I simply could not comprehend the exact figuring in algebra with the OCD also stuck in my mind. I was taking ancient history and I couldn't take down all the notes given because I kept making mistakes because of the compulsions. To make matters worse, my math teacher was still breathing down my neck about every mistake that I made. As the dictator of discipline, he punished me whenever he felt like it.

November 1989

My medicine was making me extremely drowsy. Here was the perfect chance for my English teacher to get mad at me. I was up at the back of the room one day when she was lecturing on *A Tale of Two Cities*, which of course is considered to be a classic. I found it confusing with too many sub-plots and characters that only showed up for a while. An eighteenth-century soap opera. Anyway, I accidentally fell asleep and woke up about 20 minutes later. Naturally, everyone was staring at me. "I'm sorry, Mrs. ... (I can't mention her name.) "It was probably my medication," I said as soon as I realized what had just happened. "Well, next time try not to fall asleep," she retorted sarcastically in her evil, frog-like voice.

December 1989

Holiday season was rapidly approaching, which meant good news and bad news. The good news: my sister was coming up from Maryland. The bad news: my sister was coming up from Maryland. My sister could always find a way to both cheer me up and depress me. But, I thought, this is great. I'll get to see my brother-in-law and my 3-month-old nephew, and I'd get to hang around with my sister for a while. Unfortunately, from the moment my sister entered the house, chaos ensued. Tension was building up inside of me. Tension leads to anxiety. Anxiety leads to sudden outbursts of compulsions. I was touching walls, doors, hallways, things lying around on the tables. New obsessions were entering my mind. Eventually, my brother-in-law came up and mellowed things out. My brother-in-law has a very relaxed personality. He helped to clear things up between my sister and myself until he had to go home three days later to return to work. The night before my sister was to return home, we got involved in a huge argument. Ater she left, my mind was going crazy with compulsions that were extremely hard to fight off.

January 1990

A new decade, new hopes, new worlds to explore—same old problem. The dictator of discipline was making up stories and claiming I had done things that I had never done. I wouldn't accept the punishment and this led to even more problems at school.

February 1990

Valentine's Day is my birthday. I spent $25.00 on KISS tapes. I wanted a tattoo but my parents wouldn't go for it.

March 1990

My father's place of employment no longer existed and he became a housewife. I was kicked out of public high school, which is probably good. I was kicked out of most of my classes anyway and had more studies than classes. I was determined to destroy my obsessive-compulsive disorder. If not, I was gonna die trying. (That's inside humor.) Right now I don't know where I'm going or what the future holds in store for me, but I do know that "I'm not alone when I'm strong inside." And I think maybe this time, I'm gonna be all right.

Michael A.
Excerpts from a personal diary
kept between the ages of 13 and 15 years
Massachusetts

SARA'S STORY

I would be very interested in contributing my account of my battle with OCD. In the reading I have done, I haven't come across any story quite like mine. It would have helped me if I had. Perhaps my account could help someone else.

I've had OCD since I was a child. I used to turn light switches off and on a certain number of times; count various things such as steps, words, letters; check and double check and triple check; touch corners, etc. Some rituals changed as I got older; some got dropped, others were added. I kept it as well hidden as possible. I remember once, as a child, I had started turning light switches off and on twice. Gradually the number increased to 20 times. By then it was obvious to my family. My mother got mad one day and I dropped it back to two times. It wasn't until the late 1980's that I learned that this was a disease. That was when I first heard of Clomipramine. I didn't look into it because I thought that I had a mild case and was always able to keep it fairly under control and hidden.

I gave birth to my daughter, my only child, in March of 1991. Within six days, I sank into a severe depression and was having strange and violent obsessive thoughts about my daughter. I didn't know what was happening. I wanted her and loved her and couldn't understand where these thoughts were coming from. It started as a fear that I would deliberately drop her. Because of this, I was afraid to pick her up. Within a week or so it grew into a fear that I would harm her in other ways, specifically stab her, which has always been a fear I'd had—being stabbed by someone. I felt that I had completely lost my identity. I didn't believe in killing bugs! Where were these thoughts coming from? I thought that I was either losing my mind or that I was possessed. I started seeing a psychologist when I was pregnant due to fears of having a miscarriage, having had two in the past. I told him everything. He didn't think it meant much except that I was just overwhelmed with my new responsibility. The severe depressions and obsessions continued for three months. In June we were all in a car accident caused by a drunk driver. None of us was physically injured, but I got much worse. The first week after the accident I was wrapped up in the fear that I could have lost Caiti. Then the obsessions came back stronger than ever. I couldn't stop the thoughts, the anxiety. I was so afraid constantly. I felt so guilty that I could have such horrible thoughts about my baby daughter. I felt like I was caught in a trap with no way out. If only I had never had a bad thought about her. If only I could do it all over again. I would live the rest of my life in shame for having such thoughts. I couldn't forgive myself, even if God could forgive me. I spent day after day in severe anxiety and depression, constantly examining and analyzing why I was having the thoughts. I would literally collapse at night into sleep, my only freedom. I was afraid to be alone with her but I had no choice. We were living in a small town in Montana; my family and close friends lived back east. I spent a lot of time out with her, taking walks, visiting friends, anything to avoid being alone with her. I felt that as long as someone else was around, I wouldn't go through with my obsession. I spent a lot of time crying and praying. I wanted so much to be like a normal mother. I came up with so many answers to my questions, but nothing changed. Eventually, I was going around in circles, analyzing the same questions over and over, getting the same useless answers, useless because they didn't stop the obsessions. I called religious groups asking for prayer. My husband tried so hard to understand but didn't know what to do with me. My psychologist didn't believe in medication. He suggested "thought stopping" and "keeping busy." I was breast feeding and my husband didn't want me to take medication because I would have to stop breast feeding which he thought was important. More than once I cried with my therapist telling him how scared I was that I would eventually follow through with the obsession, either because the thoughts would talk me into it or as a way to end the thoughts. He didn't believe that I would do anything. He tried reassuring me constantly. It didn't help.

One day in September, while my mother was visiting, we were getting ready to take a walk. I was alone in the kitchen holding my daughter. She was 5 ½ months old. I suddenly decided that maybe I could stop the obsessions by proving to myself that I couldn't do what I feared. I thought I was making myself have the thoughts on purpose at times, trying to convince myself over and over again that I couldn't do it. Because of the thoughts, I couldn't trust my self any more. I felt out of control of my thoughts and was afraid that I would also lose control of my behavior. I walked over to the counter while holding my daughter. I picked up a knife from the counter and held it next to my daughter. I immediately covered the blade with my hand and put the knife away. I told my mother what I had done. She said that I could stop the obsession now, since I had proven to myself that I couldn't do it. Of course that didn't work. I didn't realize that I wasn't causing the obsessions myself. I was on the verge of a total breakdown. My mother suggested that I take a medication she had, Klonopin, to calm down. It worked within 30 minutes. I became calm. The obsessions stopped. I told my psychologist and he gave in and got me a prescription for Klonopin. For a time, I thought it was gone, though some depression was still present. The anxiety was controlled and the obsessions were less.

In January of 1992, the anxiety and obsessions started to resurface. (I later learned that Klonopin is only a short-term answer to anxiety.) A friend had some self-help books concerning the inner child. I started reading these thinking that maybe my daughter's birth had brought up some of my own childhood issues that hadn't been resolved. I made a mistake in trying to work these out on my own. Fortunately, my friend Patti was there to help and support me at that time. I continued along this line for two or three months. I began getting severely depressed again. I looked to self-help books, philosophy books, religious books, everything. I only got worse.

In the meantime, my daughter first showed signs of a seizure disorder in March, at almost a year old. In April, while we were visiting in New Mexico, we had to take her to an emergency room because of a second seizure. Many tests were run, but no answers were found. I then began to be afraid of being alone with her again because of the seizures. My obsessions got worse. One day in April, I began considering suicide as a way to stop the obsessions. I called my psychologist and begged him to give me an anti-depressant. I was in conflict about taking medication because I felt I should be able to control my own thoughts and behavior. However, I couldn't control my thoughts and therefore felt I had to try medication, though in a way, I felt like a failure by giving in to it. For some reason I hadn't felt as guilty in taking the Klonopin. My psychologist had Trazodone prescribed for me. I took it for 10 days and had bad reactions such as extreme irritability, anxiety, and hyperactivity. I then finally saw a psychiatrist who wrote me a prescription for Anafranil. I was afraid to take it. In the past I had taken Lithium for depression and Prozac to help with my eating disorder. (I became bulimic 24 years ago and still fight it. I was anorexic for two years.) I had bad reactions to both drugs. I decided that maybe I should get off all drugs. I had a bad withdrawal from Trazodone. Day by day I became worse. Another friend, Charlene, had been helping me take care of my daughter during the day since I had started taking the Trazodone. She knew about the severe anxiety and depression, but didn't know about the obsessions.

At the beginning of May, my psychologist went on vacation, which turned out to be a blessing in disguise. I went into the local hospital on an emergency basis on a Saturday night. I saw a counselor who thought hospitalization might help me. She said she would talk to the Mental Health Director. I talked with my friend Charlene again on Monday and she agreed with the counselor. I talked with my brother, who happened to call, and my husband that night. I also talked with the Mental Health Director, who also felt that hospitalization was a good idea. My brother and husband were very against the idea because they were afraid that I might get hooked up to a lot of drugs and never get out of there. I was so scared after talking with them that I decided not to go through with it the next day. I know they were both scared and were trying to look out for me. The day after this, I awoke with severe anxiety and depression. When my daughter, then 13½ months old, woke up, I froze. I was scared to deal with her. I managed to get her up and get her some breakfast, after which I called Charlene and asked her to come over immediately. We talked for a while and decided to try going for a walk. When I went to get dressed, the fears and obsessions took over. I asked her to take Caiti to her home because I couldn't take care of her and didn't want her around me. She was afraid to leave me alone, but I reassured her that I would be all right. When she left, I felt scared of everything. I felt I was at a crossroads. I had two choices: hospitalization or death. I decided that I wanted to live. I called the Mental Health Director and was told that I could see her that day. Another friend took me to see her. She called the hospital and set up admission for the next day. My husband was very upset. Fortunately, his mother was able to come within two days to take care of my daughter and be a support for my husband. She stayed for two months.

It took strength that I didn't think I had to get ready to go to the hospital that day. My husband, daughter and I all went on the three-hour drive. I was petrified both when I arrived and for the next two days. My hospital experience is a story in itself. I adjusted and spent a month there. I had many experiences and a great psychiatrist, Dr. Mendenhall. I was put on Anafranil. Within two weeks the depression lifted. Although it took months for the OCD to improve, I am one of the lucky ones who has been greatly helped by Anafranil.

There is a lot more to my story, both before and since hospitalization. I must say that Anafranil was only a part of what helped me. God played the biggest part. I asked God for strength and things got harder. I asked God for peace of mind and ended up in a psychiatric ward, but I found peace of mind for the first time in my life!

I've been out of the hospital for one year and am doing and feeling better than ever. I now live in New Mexico. In fact, due to my husband's being transferred, we moved a week and a half after I left the hospital. This was another blessing in disguise. It was like starting over. Last summer, I was on 150 mg. of Anafranil. This was raised to 175 mg. in October and 200 mg. in December due to temporary setbacks. I have had no setbacks since December. I have a good psychiatrist who really understands OCD. That is so important. I only see him once a month now. I am a stronger Christian now and spend a lot of time studying and reading God's Word. I believe that healing from God can come in many ways. I don't believe that hell could be any worse than what I went through the first 13½ months of my daughter's life. I regret what I missed with her, but thank God for what I have now. I learned a lot about mental illness even though I was once a counselor. If my experience can help others, it makes it all worthwhile.

Sara
New Mexico

ANTHONY'S STORY
"Kidnapped: My Brain Held Hostage"

Where to begin—I guess I was five when I first got *that feeling*, but my OCD didn't really surface until I was seven. There are no words to describe the endless circle of pain that only someone else with OCD can relate to. Sitting here trying to put it down on paper stirs up some feelings. I really want to be able to tell my story, but I know that I won't be able to put the intensity of the pain on paper. Before I get started, I want to say that no one who suffers from this disorder is helpless or should lose hope, because whether you know it or not, you do possess the tool to break the cycle. As I said, I was five when I first felt that feeling, but that was nothing compared to the nightmare I was to face two years later. I had gone with my mother to buy a lamp, which would remind me of my nightmare every time I looked at it. We had just gotten cable TV, and when we got home my father and sister were watching "The Exorcist." Why I sat down with them to watch the movie, I don't know, but I guess it was too much to handle mentally and this triggered the OCD. I started thinking that...(I hesitated here because it is hard for me to write or say this) I just could not sleep. All that went through my mind was that I was going to get possessed. My mother kept telling me that God would never allow that to happen to me. It seems like this obsession went on forever. I developed rituals of prayers and certain ways I had to do things to reassure myself that this would not happen to me. I would come home from school (if I went that day) and start getting ready for bed. The rituals consumed so much of my time. They involved taking off my clothes and then having to fold them perfectly in the hamper. If this wasn't done right, I would have to take them out to re-fold them. This, leaving me in my underwear and tee shirt, would start the ritual of putting on my pajamas. Pinned to my tee shirt were religious medals that had to be there. Putting on the pajama pants was the easy part; it was the tee shirt that consumed most of the time. I would have to stand in front of the mirror and kiss the medals and then look at them in the mirror in four steps. As anyone with OCD knows, once is not enough.

By now I must have been about nine. Waiting patiently for me was the cage that would hold my brain hostage. The religious rituals faded, but taking their place were the thoughts of killing my family. These thoughts went round and round in my head, ripping me apart inside. OCD stole my childhood away from me.

Over the years I went through many of the OCD games (hand washing, contamination, etc.). If I accidentally bumped somebody or touched someone, in my mind I had done something that would lead to their death. My obsessions even turned me into a hypochondriac. But the thoughts of killing would somehow always find their way back into my mind. The thoughts even told me that God had put me here to kill my family, and if I didn't they would never die. I missed a lot of school. My parents were lost. They didn't know what to do. Thinking about it now, I feel they thought it was a phase that I was going through. My mother would tell me to pray and it would bring some relief, but I would start ritualizing. God became my unfailing source of strength and comfort. The OCD went into remission, leading me to believe that I had beaten this problem—it was gone and that was all that mattered. I managed to get through high school with little interference from OCD. It wasn't until after I had graduated that I found out what was wrong with me. My OCD resurfaced very strongly. Those horrible thoughts came back and now it wasn't just my family, it was anyone. I was horrified. I had thought that I had beaten this thing. I decided that I had to seek professional help. I went to my mother and asked her to help me. Mom sent me to talk to Father Leo, who agreed to find me the help that I needed. It didn't take him long and the man he found was GOD SENT. His name was Robert Redden. This man gave a name to what I had. I wasn't crazy or alone, as I had thought. I now knew what I had had all through my childhood and all I wanted was some kind of drug that would take it all away. This doctor told me that Prozac was the miracle that I wanted (Anafranil was not available in the U.S. at the time). When I first started taking Prozac, it seemed to make the thoughts more intense. By now the OCD had crippled me. Sessions with Rob were very helpful. I told him things that I had never told anyone else. Once I had told my mother about these thoughts of killing, and she told me never to tell anyone because I would be locked up. So I started to tell Rob about the thoughts that never went away, that had robbed me of my childhood and were now trying to take my adult life as well, holding my brain hostage.

At night, these thoughts became stronger. The intensity of these thoughts was crippling. I could hardly function. One second seemed like an hour and these thoughts were robbing me of my life once again. I had lost all hope. I just wanted to die, because I could never take a life—I could not live with that. God gives life and only God can take life. I felt as if I were nine years old again and living in the same nightmare. Finally, I was hospitalized. The doctors gave me Klonopin to numb the pain and the anxiety. They told me that they wanted to start me on Prozac again, and although I was reluctant, I took it. This time nothing happened—I didn't get worse or better. I was discharged and continued to take the Prozac and see Rob. Little by little, I started to come back. Rob picked me up off the ground and made me face this horrible disease. Making me face the obsessive thoughts was the best medicine; he gave me the key to unlock the cage. Unfortunately, I lost Rob due to death, but I was blessed to have known him for the time that I had. I still have my good days and my bad days. I feel that I have 95% of myself back and I refuse to let this monster (OCD) take away any more of my life. The one person who truly helped me is with God and I know that both He and Rob are watching over me. I'm 23 now and I have the will, drive and a reason to live and stay well. I start attending classes at Arkansas State University in July of 1993 where I will be majoring in English and Psychology. I want to be able to help people who are still suffering and have lost all hope. God be with you—there is peace from Obsessive-Compulsive Disorder.

Anthony
New Jersey
In loving memory of Robert Redden. May his spirit live on through his work and the people whom he touched.

LORETTE'S STORY

It's hard to know where to begin about something that takes over your life and is a part of everything you do in the course of a day.

I believe that I've always had OCD. But it really started becoming apparent at about age eleven. My bedroom was the place in which I was most a perfectionist. My clothes were all placed evenly spaced in the closet. I had some clothes which I had a hard time wearing for fear of ruining them. I had a fear of getting things out of a drawer for fear of wrecking the "order" of things. It got so that I had to do my own laundry as my mom couldn't do it right for me. I'm sure that I must have seemed like an ungrateful, hard-to-please child.

Somehow I struggled through my high school years and married shortly after graduation. Symptoms escalated; I now had a home to keep perfect. I would get everything for my husband so he wouldn't have to touch anything. It got increasingly hard to have anyone in my home; I couldn't answer the door or the phone.

After the birth of our daughter in 1977, the added stress of caring for an infant heightened symptoms again. I couldn't go out socially—I never had time. Besides, I couldn't have a baby-sitter in my house.

I would have to be up at 3:30 AM to start my daily rituals, so of course by 8:00 PM I'd be exhausted. My husband and daughter had to go to bed when I did or no one was allowed to touch anything.

Time was a big thing with me. I lived in a constant panic of trying to beat the clock. Even in sleep, I had a hard time finding rest as I was constantly looking at the clock when I'd awaken in between cat naps to make sure that I didn't oversleep; even though the alarm was set I couldn't trust it.

I could hardly cook, and by the end of a day, after my kitchen was spotless, I couldn't even walk in there. I had to do laundry at the laundrymat as I couldn't use my washer and dryer. I used a cloth to touch everything. I'd flick light switches and open and close doors a certain number of times. I was becoming more and more unable to function.

Then came the day when I turned on the TV to the Donahue Show. Dr. Judith Rappaport, along with some OCD sufferers, was on. To me, it was like someone turning on a light. I finally knew what I had. I could relate to a lot of the things that they were saying. I immediately got on the phone to call my youngest sister to tell her to watch; we were suffering from the same thing. She is a compulsive hair puller along with having other OCD symptoms, but she will tell you her own story. After that day, I began searching for help. To make a long story shorter, things began to fall into place; I started Prozac and began to get relief.

It is now four years later. I am able to have a much more normal life. I have gotten my family involved in the genetic linkage study at Columbia University in New York. We've had blood samples taken and interviews done for their study. We hope this will help.

In writing this I have re-lived a lot of old pain, cried for the lost years, the time wasted and the opportunities missed. I was unable to be a whole person, the person that I wanted to be and am now slowly becoming.

I thank my family for being there for me. For trying to understand this disorder and for all of their support.

Lorette
Canada

TRICHOTILLOMANIA! WHY?

Hiding! I think I've been hiding all my life. From what, I'm just not sure.

I'm a 35-year-old woman and I've worn a wig for 10 years. My hair pulling started at age nine with my eyelashes. Before this I was a bed-wetter. After much embarrassment and humiliation, both stopped. At puberty (which was age 11 for me), the hair pulling started and increased slowly as the years passed, until the wigs I now wear became a necessary item in my life.

A person seems to search for understanding and reasoning. As an adult, I find myself in life's fast lane. Not giving myself time to slow down for fear that I might have to search for myself, knowing that I cannot really be myself until this dreaded ritual leaves me.

Please understand: I will not be defeated as I have a husband, three daughters, a career and am involved in many community activities and organizations. I do feel that I have to work twice as hard as other people just to prove myself. In my prayers, I pray for my ritual to stop.

Dear parents, if you have a child with Trichotillomania, get medical help as soon as possible. Do not believe the doctor if he/she feels that your child will outgrow this ritual. I'm afraid that this problem will not go away by itself. It's just better hidden. I hope in reading this it will help somebody else out there.

Canada

LIZ'S STORY

Here I am, 33 years old, assistant production manager at a local broadcasting station, constantly counting, checking door locks and cleaning repeatedly. I get so mad at myself. Why am I doing these stupid things? My mind is constantly racing, memorizing numbers and counting objects. Sometimes my only relief is a migraine headache. Then I am too sick to do any rituals or care about the obsessive thoughts. I can pull the blinds, stay in bed, and just shut down.

Did you know that nobody would know this about me if I hadn't told them? I've never been caught at work or anyplace else, by co-workers or even a boyfriend, doing any stupid superstitious rituals—inserting a computer disk into the drive only to eject and re-insert it exactly four times, opening and closing my car door repeatedly until I've gotten it just right (I've thought a happy or a good thought at the right moment). There are too many superstitious rituals to be put on paper, but the bottom line is that they're silly, stupid, unnecessary things that I feel I have to do or something bad could happen.

And so, after I've confided to my parents or a friend, they have the nerve to say, "Well, why don't you just quit doing those stupid things?" That ticks me off! Maybe they just can't understand until they feel what I'm feeling. I'm frustrated and mad at myself. I'm mad at this disorder that wreaks havoc on my life.

I grew up having no idea what I was doing, only knowing that doing these stupid things would temporarily make me feel better. I didn't think I was crazy, just that I was different, that I was doing something that I didn't think anybody else did.

When I was about 10 years old, I remember my mom and a friend talking at our house about a variety of subjects, including ESP and the likelihood of UFOs. I confided for the very first time to somebody about my stupid rituals and neither one of them had much to say about it. As open-minded as I felt my mom was, after her friend left, she asked me not to bring up stupid questions and ideas like that again. It wasn't her fault. Until the last few years, I don't think anybody knew about this anxiety disorder. Thank heavens, we who have Obsessive-Compulsive Disorder know that we're not alone now.

I believe there are so many people still left undiagnosed, and I'm afraid that the majority of doctors are still clue-less about this disorder. That's scary. What's even scarier is how a doctor (many times) does not know how to say, "I don't know very much about this." If they would only try to refer us to someone who is knowledgeable about OCD; or they could try to become more knowledgeable about it themselves.

For the past three years I've been on 40mg. of Prozac and I feel so much better now. I feel like a different person. I still have my counting and superstitious rituals that I have to do, but not nearly to the extent that they were. I'd say that the obsessions and compulsions have been reduced by about 50%. I can live with that. I'm told that I could probably reduce the OCD even more if I were to seek behavior therapy along with Prozac, but I'm reluctant. I really don't want to face that anxiety any more than I have to. Besides, if it's a chemical imbalance, I would rather treat it with drugs. Some friends don't like my taking Prozac or any other drug. That makes me mad also, because they're not the ones suffering. That would be like telling diabetics that they don't need insulin shots.

In summary, I'm frustrated at times and hate the anxiety I feel if I don't do the rituals. But I'm thankful that we're learning more about OCD and I'm also thankful that we have drugs like Prozac available to us; it's changed my life for the better.

Liz
Missouri

CONNIE W.'S STORY

For me, living with OCD is a life (if this is what you want to call it) full of loneliness, guilt, worthlessness, frustration, depression;but hardest of all, it is living a secret life that no one could possibly even begin to understand. I am 43 years old now, and have had OCD since my early 20's. I feel tired and stressed all the time. This disease makes my every move a chore—an exceptionally big chore, knowing that everything I do must always be *perfect*! If it isn't done to (my definition of) perfection, then I am extremely anxious and feel that I am a failure. I am not allowed to sit down and enjoy myself in anything until I am totally exhausted from cleaning everything to my perfection. A workday for me meant getting up three hours before I was to leave, then sleeping on the bus and the train to relax a little, sometimes taking naps instead of coffee breaks and lunches to get me through the day, again sleeping on the ride home and dreading the next three-hour ritual. Then I have to decide whether to eat some dinner (on an already upset stomach) and take the chance of being sick, or just go to bed and eat something when the hunger pains wake me up in the middle of the night. Friday nights were for food shopping, the bank and any other stores that I needed to go to. Saturday was cleaning, cooking and wash day. Sunday was spending half the day taking care of my personal needs and the other half was my "social life," which consisted of television or sleeping to help my tired, worn body.

I am now home on disability due to severe osteoporosis, a left total hip replacement, post broken right leg, severe nerve damage in my lower back and down my left leg, and two extremely bad feet with a fracture in the right one. But, you know what? If I had a choice, I would take all the pain over my OCD any day. Unfortunately, I don't have that choice and must live with both. At least I don't have to keep the physical pain that I have a secret; and that is the worst pain of all—living with the awful secret of having OCD.

Thanks to this book, I hope we all make a friend or two. Much love and strength to my friends,

Connie W.
Pennsylvania

DEBBIE'S STORY

Before I begin to share my story I want to encourage the reader not to give up the fight in the battle against OCD. There is more information on OCD now than there was a decade ago. There is hope.

When I saw the notice in the OCD newsletter, I knew I had to respond. If my story can help or encourage just one other person, it will be worth it all. Let me also say that it is difficult to disclose my story, because it causes me to relive the extremely difficult times. It has been a nightmare at times. OCD is a very crippling disease; it affects the sufferer and also family members. It is very much a hidden disease. I did not want to share it with anyone lest they think I was crazy. Even going to a psychiatrist for help, I was afraid to share my symptoms because I thought the doctor would think I was crazy.

I am 35 years of age and my symptoms first arose when I was age 12. It began with intrusive thoughts like, "What if I hurt a family member?" At that young age, I was scared silly at thinking such strange thoughts. I remember my dad reassuring me that it was just "thoughts." As the years went by, any time in my life when I was under stress, the intrusive thoughts would enter my mind. In 1976 I entered college away from home and had to withdraw after three weeks because the intrusive thoughts were so disabling. After withdrawing from college I had my first of many visits to psychiatrists. I never heard the psychiatrist mention OCD; his treatment was psychoanalysis and medications, none of which helped but caused severe side effects.

Eight years later I began to have a problem with fear of contamination and dirt and began the ritual of hand-washing. I then began to see a behavioral therapist and started taking another medication for anxiety. This was not helpful in alleviating the OCD.

Because I do not have unlimited space in which to share my story, I need to be brief. During the time from 1976 to 1991, I saw over twenty different psychiatrist and psychologists, only two of which ever mentioned OCD. I have tried or been on medications including Elavil, Stelazine, Haldol, Desyrel, Zanax, Norpramin, Tofranil, Anafranil, and Prozac (pill form). None of these medications ever made a substantial difference.

In 1988 I moved from the northeast to Texas—a very difficult move for me. Intrusive thoughts began to escalate. Life was miserable. I felt anxious and depressed most of the time. My husband tried to be as supportive as he could but I knew he didn't understand all that I was going through.

In January of 1990, I had a beautiful baby girl. I was very apprehensive of how I would handle motherhood plagued by intrusive thoughts. At this time I did get a prescription from a psychiatrist for Anafranil. I had read about Anafranil in the OCD newsletter which I had been receiving. It was not an effective medication for me. The psychiatrist who prescribed Anafranil would not work with me in trying another drug—it was Anafranil or nothing. I was beginning to feel very helpless. Fall and Spring of 1991 were very difficult. I couldn't lift or carry my daughter without extreme pain in my legs due to the complications of a car accident in 1983. Severe back and leg pain coupled with increasing intrusive thoughts had me almost non-functional physically and emotionally. After consulting with two more psychiatrists, one who recommended a *vitamin approach* (he is a well known psychiatrist), I was at rock bottom. I could not sleep or eat due to the emotional stress of intrusive thoughts. Life was miserable. I needed a miracle, and immediately. I was looking through an OCD newsletter and saw a doctor listed by the name of Dr. Claghorn in Houston. I did not want to travel to another psychiatrist; I was so worn out. But I knew I couldn't just give up. He recommended trying liquid Prozac since I had had a bad experience several times trying Porzac in pill form. I was not happy with his recommendation. I asked him about therapy, and he said that for intrusive thoughts such as I have, liquid Prozac was the treatment of choice. I didn't end up taking the liquid Prozac until six weeks later. I was very leery about taking another drug that I was sure would give me side effects. Finally, I was so desperate that I thought, "What have I got to lose?", and with the encouragement of another physician, I started taking it. What a difference! I noticed a big improvement. I was sleeping again at night; I could eat again; I felt relaxed for the first time in my life. Most of the anxiety I had always felt was gone. The intrusive thoughts subsided and when they did enter my mind they were fleeting thoughts. It has been two and one half years now since I have been taking liquid Prozac. I feel like a new person. Life is just beginning. I thank God every day for liquid Prozac—for me it is the **Miracle Drug!** Also, thanks to Dr. Claghorn in Houston, Texas. I have recently received a Ph.D. in counseling psychology, and my goal is to help OCD sufferers.

Don't give up the fight!

Debbie M.
Texas

A FATHER'S STORY

In April of 1989, after many years of suffering and pain, my 25-year-old daughter took her own life by swallowing an overdose of pills. Behind that simple statement lies a complex story. It is my belief that the responsibility for her death is shared by a fatally flawed mental health system and the terrible disease that she suffered. That disease was a severe Obsessive-Compulsive Disorder. In my daughter's case, this meant obsessive thoughts that at their worst dominated her day. She was certain that her thoughts could harm people, even fatally, by her merely talking with them on the phone. These obsessive thoughts resulted in compulsive behavior rituals to ward off the terrible consequences. If even one tiny thing went wrong in her washing ritual she would have to start all over. This would often result in showers that lasted four to six hours. She could not smoke a cigarette unless it was fitted exactly into the center of her mouth; otherwise it was discarded and a fresh one took its place. She was compelled to walk down the center of the sidewalk or a hallway, and if she were prevented from doing that she either had to start all over, or step aside and wait for a clear path. Her obsessive thoughts and compulsive behavior totally dominated her existence toward the end and completely took over every aspect of her daily life, from eating to dressing, from reading and writing to interacting with others.

I believe that along with the disease the responsibility for her death is shared by a large number of mental health care professionals who treated her during more than a decade of her illness, including:

An arrogant psychiatrist who was so confident of himself and so ignorant that he diagnosed my daughter as psychotic and prescribed a psychotropic drug after just a 40-minute interview with her. This same psychiatrist lied to my daughter and tried to get us to lie to her about his plans for long-term hospitalization for her by telling her he just wanted to hospitalize her "for some tests." The tests took two weeks. She was in the hospital for three months.

A Licensed Clinical Social Worker who was so inept and at the same time so insecure that she could not deal with even the slightest sign of skepticism from us. She could only cry out in frustration and defensiveness, "Don't you think I know how to 'do' therapy?"

A kindly but ineffectual psychiatrist who was totally confused about what to do for his patient.

A psychiatrist who ran a psychiatric wing of a children's hospital with his favorite theory as his controlling device. He dismissed many obvious signs and clues to my daughter's obsessive-compulsive illness (even those provided by his own department of psychological testing) that could have helped him to help her.

He dismissed them because he tried to fit everything into the envelope that he called "Take the child out of the stress caused by the home and parents, and she will find the freedom from stress that will automatically lead to mental health."

A county mental health psychiatrist who, as a treatment for my daughter's alcoholism (one of her more destructive ways of dealing with the devastating mental pain and anguish of OCD), was willing to warehouse her in a locked custodial ward rather than sending her to an alcohol rehabilitation facility.

Another Licensed Clinical Social Worker who was so threatened and confused by my daughter's manipulative attempts to get herself discharged from a hospital where she had been sent deceitfully that she unilaterally "committed" her without a second thought to an extremely dangerous and violent ward in a state hospital.

A well-meaning older psychologist who insisted that we must provide employment for our daughter to build her sagging ego, even if we had to pay someone on the "QT" to pretend to hire her.

A psychiatrist who shouted at and pushed our daughter around and urged us to do the same to "teach her a lesson" about who was in charge.

A very self-confident social worker who, during my daughter's last months of life, diagnosed her obsessive thoughts as nothing more than an over-active photographic memory one week, and then the next week decided that her fear of harming people through her obsessive thoughts was because she was psychic. This same social worker, after seeing a TV special on OCD, proclaimed to us, "Now I know what her illness is." Our daughter had told her about the OCD problem, as had we, but only TV could get through to her. This same social worker used dangerously poor judgement. We gave her our daughter's OCD medication, on which she had overdosed more than once while drunk, on her promise that she would administer and monitor it. Instead, when our daughter stopped seeing her she gave the medication to her unstable companion.

A psychiatrist who decided on his first and only visit with my daughter that her problem could be solved with mega-vitamins.

A psychologist who after a single session with my daughter (and me) decided that what she was missing was closeness with the family. He therefore told us that henceforth I was to take my daughter out to dinner on a regular basis, starting that very day at the end of our session.

The staffs of three different mental health hospitals. After each hospitalization she was much worse than when she was admitted.

All of the above-listed people are real, separate people. They are not composites. They are not fictional characters.

None of these people had a clue as to the real problem that my daughter was facing, the obsessive-compulsive disorder that would ultimately destroy her.

None of these people know about this disorder, and I blame them all for not knowing. During the 10 years that my daughter was desperately seeking help for this illness, it was already being treated with the drug Anafranil (Chlomipramine) in Canada, Mexico, and some countries of Europe with a good degree of success, and had been for nearly 10 years. None of them kept up with the psychiatric journals of these countries, or even with the *Journal of the American Psychiatric Association*, which made some information available.

We will always be grateful for the honesty of just one county psychiatrist who recognized the disease and was frank enough to admit that he could not be of any help at all—one partially-informed, straight-forward therapist out of twelve or more from whom she sought treatment.

By the time we had, on our own, researched this illness and the drug Anafranil and gotten help from a psychiatrist in Canada, my daughter's disease had progressed so far that it would ultimately destroy her. At those times in her treatment period when her lifestyle would allow her to take Anafranil regularly, Monica felt that the drug was beginning to help her. We had allowed ourselves to hope that if the oral Anafranil treatment had not been adequate to relieve her symptoms, she would consider residential intravenous Anafranil treatment in Canada. Her life was to become so troubled, confused and hellish that she would take her own life before she could even really consider that.

I blame all the professionals who worked with us for not knowing more when that knowledge was available. I blame my daughter as well for the unhelpful ways that she sometimes handled things (which were often, but not always, out of her control), and I blame myself for not finding out more sooner.

In a time when many of our political and health care leaders are proclaiming the superiority of health care in the United States and defaming such health systems as the Canadian system, it is very painful and ironic for us to remember that the only real help we were able to get for our daughter was from a Canadian psychiatrist. It is painful and tragic for us to remember that our health system in the United States failed our daughter and was a major contributing factor in her death. It could have been a major factor instead in the saving of her life had its practitioners even been aware of what other, "poorer" national health systems had already discovered and been practicing for years.

It is hard for us to be overly grateful for our country's health system, purported to be the best and most advanced in the world. We remember too much. We carry too much in our hearts. We will never be able to forget any of it.

Ralph R. Prime
California

MY CHILD, THEN AND NOW

I
Package
Of fresh sunshine.
Too full to be
Contained in her own box
Spills her bright jewel laughter
On us all.

II
I see her as I fear she'll be,
A cold and lifeless form.
A death so real it frightens me
And makes me want to warm
Her being and her heart.

Yet it is not for me to stay
The certainty of death.
(and death will come unless a way
is found to give her breath)
But she must make a start.

What she once was might come again
But only by her grace.
She cannot live just now and then
And run the human race.
Surviving is the art.

I have but little hope,
I here confess despair.

Ralph R. Prime

KAYDEE'S STORY
"Have I Worried Enough?"

I can remember my first attack like it was yesterday. I had gone for a walk around the town (just a small city area) and I took along a stick that I had picked up from somewhere. Halfway through the walk, I decided that I no longer wanted to carry the stick, so I threw it away. Suddenly, after getting home, I just KNEW that my brother's high school class ring was attached to the stick, and I had thrown it away. I thought about it and kept saying to my self, "Maybe it wasn't," "it was," "I just knew it," "I knew it" over and over; it was all I could think about. I was in a panic. I went back to get the stick because I thought this would make everything right; but it didn't. I worried about it over and over. I had to tell my mother what had happened. She asked me why I had taken the ring. I told her that I didn't take it, it was just on the stick. She looked for the ring. It was on the mantel where my brother left it. I still knew that I had lost something valuable. I just didn't know what.

Then I turned into a washer—my hands had to be clean. All I had to do was wash them when I thought they were dirty. If I touched my mouth, I would have to wash my hands. I would think, "Did I wash my hands?" Maybe I should wash them now in case I hadn't. I would try not to touch people if I thought my hands weren't clean. I was afraid that I would make them sick and that they would die. When I went to church, I would not want to shake hands with people. I remember one evening when I came home, my mother had made chicken. I reached into the pot and broke off a piece. How could I have made such a mistake? I believed that I had contaminated the whole pot. I thought I would make everyone sick if they ate it. What could I do? I had to tell my brother what had happened. How could he be so calm? Didn't he understand? Something awful was about to happen.

Then there was the mushroom. I was walking behind the church near the woods when I saw a mushroom. I kicked it, the top broke off, and I noticed that it was all black inside. Oh no! It's poisonous and now the poison was in the air! What could I do now? Could I stop the poison? I decided to put the top back on the mushroom; that would stop the poison from getting into the air. I had touched it and so now my hands were tainted with the poison. I had to wash them. I went to the side of the church where there was a water faucet and rinsed off my shoe, careful not to spread any more poison. I washed my hands and then I thought, "Now the water supply would be contaminated and thousands of people would die!" What could I do? There was no way to stop it! I expected the morning news to say, "Thousands Die—Water Supply Tainted." It of course didn't happen, but nonetheless I did not stop washing. I worried that when I washed my hands that the contaminants were being let into the water supply and could not be filtered out. People would die and it would be my fault.

The washing was replaced by checking. I would think that the water was still running after I had washed my hands. It became much easier not to wash my hands instead of worrying about the running water. I was unable to tell anyone; I knew they would not understand. My mother said that I would grow out of it.

I took an electronics class in high school in which we would would etch circuit boards. I was afraid of the etching solution because it was poisonous. What if I got some on my skin and did not know it? Would it hurt me or someone that I came into contact with? I would worry about leaving the boards in the solution too long, because it could completely dissolve them. I thought, "What if I left the water running after rinsing the boards? What if the drain were stopped up?" I just knew the water was filling up the electronics lab and everything would be ruined. I even called the school because I didn't want to worry all weekend. It was hard to do, because I was the only girl who took electronics and they would know who it was. The office secretary answered and told me that the teacher had already left. I told her that I thought that I had left the water running and wanted to know if she could check it. She told me that she felt the teacher would have checked it before leaving. This was not reassuring at all!

My first year of college was enjoyable. I was well known by the faculty and staff members. My grades were very good and I was in the Honor Society. I felt really good for once, and even laughed about the mushroom story with a classmate. I thought that my mother had been right—I had outgrown it.

This didn't last into my second year. I knew that the time would come for me to look for a job. I applied at many of the local industries; however, my confidence was lacking. When the phone didn't ring, or "We just hired someone yesterday" happened, I just stopped trying. I went to work at a restaurant after graduating.

I continued to go to college as a part-time student. After working at the restaurant for a year and a half, I found a job as a drafter. Washing the ink from my pens worried me; I thought that the ink might poison the drinking water. I also took outrageous precautions with the cleaning solution for the drafting table. I still have this solution today (four years later) because I worry about disposing of it safely.

I seem to worry about such silly things and can't stop myself. I try to think of other things, but the worries still come back. I can't stop them; all I can do is worry about them. It's not fair! I don't want to live like this. Why can't I just be happy sometimes, instead of worrying all the time?

I now work at a pharmacy where I can find lots of things to worry about! I couldn't touch the prescriptions as I worried that I would cause someone to die. What could I do at three in the morning, worrying that I had given someone the wrong prescription. Could I call the pharmacist and tell him that I thought I may have killed someone? He would think I was crazy. Maybe I am crazy. Maybe this is what it's like. No free time in your mind, worrying all the time, always thinking "What if?". Never able to be sure.

I couldn't do anything without weighing all the consequences. What if someone got hurt? I was at the point where I didn't think that I could continue; my mind seemed so confused. There was no one that I could talk to about it; I didn't think anyone would understand. I did talk with a pharmacist often, telling him what I thought about. One day he said, "It sounds like obsessive-compulsive disorder." I didn't know what it was so I went to the library and checked out books on anxiety. One of them had a little information on OCD; however, it was enough to convince me of what I was suffering from. I went to a doctor and told her that I thought I had OCD. Her opinion was that I was depressed (who wouldn't be if they had OCD and didn't know it?). I started taking Anafranil and seeing a therapist (he too thought I was depressed). I now am much happier and have even stopped checking most of the time.

It's a wonderful feeling!!

I would like to share this part of my life so that others may be able to understand what it is like to be ruled by worry.

Kaydee
Virginia

CÉCILE'S STORY

My name is Cécile. I'm 33 years old. I've lived with OCD since the age of 15. In September of '74, I was symptom-free, but by Christmas, OCD had embedded itself in my life. No one could wash my clothes or bedding but me; I couldn't lend or borrow clothes, either. I couldn't stand wearing something that had touched someone else. I stopped hanging out with friends. I was so ashamed of my behavior and knew it was odd. I didn't want anyone to find out how weird I was. I especially avoided boys. I couldn't be touched. If anyone touched my hair or my skin, I felt "contaminated" and had to "disinfect" myself. My family didn't know what was happening to me. They knew only that I was spending more and more time in the bathroom. Many arguments erupted as a result of this. Showering alone could take up to 30 minutes or more. My mother would yell at me for wasting so much water. I couldn't dry my hands on the same towel as everyone else, so I used Kleenex or toilet paper. That also caused problems because toilet paper especially disappeared at an alarming rate, as did soap.

Looking back, I don't know how I got through college and university, except that I was studying psychology and hoped to cure myself. My first year at university was my first time away from home. I had my own apartment and my freedom. Within a couple of months I began to diet, and by the end of that first year, I was anorexic. To this day, I'm preoccupied with my weight and control my daily caloric intake. Eventually, I dropped out of psychology. I felt I was too emotionally disturbed to help anyone. I studied literature and translation. Finally, at the age of 26, I sought professional help in the form of a psychiatrist. I've been in therapy ever since. I was so ashamed of my OCD that I didn't begin talking about it until my second year of therapy. Now I'm very much at ease talking about it with my therapist. Unfortunately, my therapy hasn't led to any significant improvement in my condition. Two years ago, I decided to try medication. I was on Anafranil (Chlomipramine) for eight months. I didn't notice any real change in my behavior. After four months off medication, I started taking Prozac (Fluoxetine). Presently, I'm taking 60 mg. a day. I'm discouraged because this drug isn't helping me either. In fact, I feel more depressed than ever and find getting through each day exhausting. I haven't worked in over a year, and even when I was working—as a freelance translator—it was from my home. I've always avoided contact with people and the "real" world as much as possible. Now, I can't even imagine working because I have no energy, no interest in anything. I'm relieved to be sharing an apartment with my sister because she could support me financially if it came to that, and it might. Sometimes I just want to live out my life in this apartment and not struggle any more. There are also times when I contemplate suicide because I can't bear the thought of living my whole life with OCD. I know that as long as I have OCD, I'll never have friends—and certainly not an intimate relationship with a man.

Cécile B.
Québec Province
Canada

"DON'T LAUGH WHEN YOU NEED TO CRY...
BUT DON'T FORGET TO LAUGH

I want to credit Melody Beattie for the title of this piece. I found the quote on one of her co-dependent calendars and it really spoke to me. When I was hospitalized in 1982 at the age of 29 with severe OCD, believe me, nothing was funny. I had completely lost my sense of humor, a sense of humor that had grown and developed over many years of my Jewish heritage. Everybody in my family was funny, with a dry, intellectually, yet bizarre wit. I remember watching Jonathan Winters on television in the late 50's and 60's and thinking he was the funniest man on earth! I still feel that way. Mort Sahl, George Carlin, Bill Cosby, and Woody Allen all became my idols at a very young age. Humor was everything in our house—we laughed more than we cried. When my OCD hit, the laughter left. Nothing, and I mean nothing, was funny. My life was so out of balance that I became incapable of seeing the abstract in life, something that was second nature to me before the illness.

It's now almost eleven years later. I've gone through intense therapies ranging from individual to Twelve-Step programs, cognitive therapy, and support groups. I've returned to my love of film-making to write and direct *The Touching Tree*—truly my own story about OCD. Most important of all, I've come to realize how important humor and lightness is in recovery from OCD or any illness. I believe humor, laughter, lightness are medicine. That doesn't mean I'm cracking jokes constantly, but what it does mean is a return to that part of my life spirit that saw the levity in life, the abstract in life, the fun in life, the balance of it all!

One of the first times I became willing to lighten up and find some humor in my own illness came about two years after I came out of the hospital. Part of my OCD revolves around germ and contamination phobias. My recovery has been mostly behavior therapy—what I call "risking." That is, to risk feeling my fears and coming out the other side "Okay." Well, I decided to feel my fear around cooking. I used to cook before OCD hit but the fear of germs stopped all that. One night, I decided to bake a chicken. I bought the chicken at a nearby store. Then it was time for the hard part—cleaning it! I had a memory of how to do it, but my OCD fears were "up" and ready for a fight. I washed that chicken for about ninety minutes! I could just imagine that poor chicken thinking "What the hell is with this guy? Does he have OCD or what?!" Finally, I got it into the oven and baked it. To this day, I continue to be proud of myself for breaking through that fear. Today, I'm able to cook. I still have fears, but that chicken taught me a lot. Of course, when I go into grocery stores, the frozen chickens look at each other and say, "Here he comes!"

Recovery is about pushing through fears, and recovery is about reclaiming what God gave us all, a spirit of humor and lightness, sometimes even when it seems dark. Today, I'm grateful to be able to laugh again. Keep the faith!

James Callner
Awareness Films
435 Alberto Way #3
Los Gatos, CA 95032

Author's note: Mr. Callner is the writer/director of *The Touching Tree.*

SUSIE'S STORY

Once upon a time there was a little girl named Susie. She was bright, attractive and talented. She graduated high school with honors and the yearbook entitled her "most likely to succeed." Indeed, just about everything Susie attempted was a success. Success, of course, is open to interpretation. For Susie, success involved establishing a healthy relationship, getting married, and parenting children. As usual, Susie managed to achieve her goals until *that* year when everything changed—

That year something was wrong.

That year Susie began to repeat a ritual she could not control.

That year she was diagnosed with Obsessive—Compulsive Disorder.

That year she was drugged, hospitalized and counseled.

That year, as she desperately sought help, no one seemed to know what to do or even how to treat OCD.

That year was 1982.

Within three years Susie watched her success crumble as she lost control of her life, lost her husband, lost her children, lost her home, lost her financial security, and basically lost her sense of self.

For the next five years Susie struggled to hold onto menial jobs as the OCD flared further out of control. Susie had no skills and was receiving no financial assistance. Local apartments were expensive, so she lived with various friends in order to stay close to the children she so dearly loved. Time passed—more counselors, more pills, more hospitals—but Susie wasn't getting any better.

In 1987 Susie made a bold decision to go to college in spite of counselors who told her it was too soon. It had been 15 years since high school and little of the self confidence that Susie had once taken for granted still remained. Could she still study, take tests, or even adjust to college life? Who knew? All Susie knew was that she had to try. Two semesters passed—4.0 GPA. Was the old Susie back? Part of her was but the OCD continued its relentless attacks as graduation neared. Susie fought back with everything she had and got her degree with high honors, but Susie never saw the ceremonies that would have honored her. She was far too ill to even attend. She was too ill, in fact, to do much of anything as the ritualistic behavior consumed more and more of her life.

Now there was *no* money, no job and nowhere to live. Welfare? "No. You still own half of the house your ex-husband and children live in." Food Stamps? "No." (Same reason.) Medicaid? "Yes, but you will have to find agencies that accept this coverage." 1989 was a time of new counselors, lesser hospitals, and generic drugs. The old ones were only covered by "good" insurance. The new agency sent Susie to "day treatment." From 9am to 3pm Susie would learn how to sew on buttons, buy and cook food, and use a checkbook. Didn't they know she was a college graduate? Didn't they know that she had run a household for 10 years and knew this stuff? How had her life deteriorated to this level? How could she even use a checkbook if there weren't any money?

Five months later Susie qualified for Social Security Disability (SSI). SSD, a better benefit, was not available because she had not "worked enough quarters in her lifetime." What about the 10 years of parenting and homemaking? "Sorry, Susie, your husband paid in but you did not. Take the SSI and *be grateful.*"

It's 1993 now and Susie still takes the SSI. She is still grateful. She still spends a lot of time with her children. She still goes to hospitals and counseling that are covered by Medicaid. They still give her drugs that don't help. They still don't seem to know much about OCD.

Somewhere inside of Susie there is still potential waiting to be tapped. There is still a spark of what made her shine in high school. There is a definite unwillingness to accept the fate that has been dealt to her.

Susie now knows that clinics exist across this nation that help people with OCD. Susie also knows that they don't accept Medicaid.

Please, someone, HELP SUSIE, and thank you for caring enough to read this.

Susie
Alden, New York

MIKE'S STORY

My name is Mike, and I grew up in a small, working-class town in Rhode Island. I have had OCD since I was 15½ years old, although I've just come to realize this within the last year and a half. I've just celebrated my 42nd birthday recently.

For more than 25 years I have been plagued by obsessional thoughts, compulsions, anxiety, and periodically, severe depressions. As OCD usually waxes and wanes over time, I have had good productive years between the bad times.

I have a wonderful wife and three children, have had some very good jobs, and even managed to earn a B.A. and an M.A. (in counselor education) from Rhode Island College. This all may sound wonderful, but during the "bad times" with OCD I have had problems in my marriage, left good jobs when the doubts and anxiety became too great, and have yet to use my degree in my field of study.

I currently drive a tractor-trailer for my work and have for sixteen years. I've been able to do this type of work because during the bad OCD times, it affords me the time to work through obsessional thoughts, and the privacy of working alone helps me control anxiety. It is a low stress job to me, so it has worked well as far as earning a living while dealing with this crippling disorder. I still consider myself lucky to be able to do this because many people with OCD aren't able to work when the "bad OCD times" occur.

It's hard to explain to most people what it is like to suffer with OCD because it is abnormal; it sounds crazy to those who don't have it, and so we tend to be very secretive and just live alone with our deep fears and depression. How can you tell someone things like: I have to keep counting to 10 or have things I am counting or figuring always end in a 10 with nothing left over or I just don't feel right, it feels uneven or out of balance to me; tell them that when you touch something with your right hand that you also MUST do the same with your left hand or you will feel somehow out of balance; tell them how you sometimes become fraught with anxiety because you think over and over "What if I lost control of myself and hurt someone else or myself?" What would most people think if you told them that you have spent much of your private thinking time trying to understand why the world is the way it is, what is the meaning of life, what is the right way to be a person, just plain "why" about everything, and you were so obsessed with "why" that you MUST get the answers, you can't stop, you MUST figure it out! Of course knowing "why" about so much is impossible and is never-ending, but, to a person with OCD it's easy to spend hours, days, months, and years worrying about seemingly insignificant things because he or she feels they MUST get the answers or something terrible might happen to them.

I could write pages and pages of different things that I have been obsessed with over the years, but the results are always the same. There is always some doubt, or "what if?" or maybe left over to start my obsessing anew in a tireless cycle. This "disorder of doubt" can certainly make people's lives torturous and make them believe that they are "crazy" or "insane" and cause deep depression.

I have been in therapy many times over the years and have earned an M.A. in the field of Psychology and Counseling trying to get the answers to feel better; but still the doubts, that maybe I didn't learn enough, would continue. Finally, thanks to my wife, I read an article on OCD written by a person with OCD who belongs to the Obsessive Compulsive Foundation. From the OCF I received a lot of information on OCD and was finally referred to a specialist in my area.

I now am taking 250 mg. of Anafranil daily (Prozac didn't work for me) with minimal side effects. If has finally helped me to ease my anxiety, has helped ease the endless doubting I would experience, and has given me some peace in my life. I am greatly improved, but know that I will never be OCD-free. I am happy to feel better, to know that I wasn't crazy, to stop feeling the tremendous guilt and depression I felt because I couldn't seem to get my life and emotions in order. I finally realized that I am a victim of genetics and not some kind of human failure.

I look forward to the rest of my life with my wife and children now, and maybe someday I will use my education and become a counselor. If not, that's OK, because I now understand that my OCD could act up again. I will find peace and happiness just knowing that I am not alone and there are people who are willing to support each other and help each other through the bad times; also, that by being honest and open we can help the researchers and professionals find more answers to solve this disabling disorder.

Occasionally I can't help but reflect on the years and opportunities lost when I didn't know what was wrong with me. I was an excellent student, class president, and have been told that I could have gone to college on an athletic scholarship. My life seemed perfect until that time when I began the obsessive-compulsive thoughts while in high school. I thought I was going crazy and lost all confidence and self-esteem. I couldn't tell anyone why I was afraid; they would put me away in the mental hospital! I knew my thoughts were absurd and abnormal, but I couldn't tell my parents. They would have been horrified and greatly disappointed that they could have a child with such a problem. Unfortunately, because of this, I couldn't concentrate on school work and felt like such a terrible failure to everyone. I started to act out how I was feeling. I became a poor student, started getting into trouble, drinking, got kicked off the sports teams; I just became the opposite of what I was and wanted to be.

When I reflect on this and other opportunities that I missed, I can't help but feel sad and angry. Even though I have accomplished a lot since those awful years in high school, I can't help but wonder how different things might have turned out if I had had supportive parents or if high school counselors could have picked up on my change in behavior, or, if as a society, we were aware of OCD.

That is why I wanted to contribute to this book. Only through information to the public and acknowledgement that many people among us may suffer from various mental problems can we then begin to find answers and offer real help. We need to stop looking at mental disorders as incurable problems which should be denied by family members and hidden away as an embarrassment never to be spoken about.

My worst moments have been when I felt totally alone with my problems, that no one could ever understood me, that I was a failure as a human being, that I was crazy.

My best moments have been when I discovered that I was not alone, that there are causes and answers to mental disorders, that they can be helped and cured if we are brave enough to open up and share our experiences.

I used to feel ashamed to admit that I have problems, but I'm happy and proud to say now that, yes, I am human and have problems, but I will face them and do what I can to help others. When we can all share our humanness with all its good and bad and ups and downs, we can become less defensive of ourselves and be closer, more helpful and happier together as a society.

Sincerely and with hope,

Mike

Rhode Island

ANNE'S STORY

I have had trichotillomania for 25 years, since I was 15 years old. For a long time I didn't know it had a name, just that it made me feel terrible and I couldn't stop.

The incident that triggered its beginning was in biology class. We were instructed to pull out one hair in order to look at the root under a microscope. After class, I kept pulling and pulling and pulling—that was the start of a lifelong cycle of knowing I should stop, but not really wanting to because it just felt good and also relieved tension.

What finally drove me to medical treatment two and a half years ago was the repeated stress of negative experiences related to this disease. I had been in and out of psychotherapy for ten years but rarely mentioned this awful compulsion to my therapist. I kept hoping I would get well, and the pulling urge would magically disappear. (Of course, it never happened.) Anafranil and Zoloft eventually helped me tremendously, but I am still not 100% symptom-free. I am also a recovering alchoholic (6 years), a nail-biter, and I crave caffeine, sugar and chocolate all the time. It seems as if I am constantly battling one bad habit or another.

This trichotillomania is definitely NOT a socially acceptable disease! Just the idea of it is repulsive to many people and that makes it even harder to seek help. In the past I spent a lot of time and anxiety on concealment and avoidance techniques rather than confronting the problem directly. I would like to share how those activities have affected my life and which weapons I now use.

As you might expect, a trip to the hairdresser's is one of the most stressful things I do. (Remember "Only her hairdresser knows for sure"?) I go, though, because I believe the results of my "episodes" would be even more obvious if I didn't. Sometimes, because of all the thin spots and bald spots, certain areas require very little trimming. And it's depressing to be faced with that fact. Similar to the alcoholic thinking in me, after every haircut I tell myself that "this time" will be different, "this time" I'll be perfectly controlled for the next six weeks, then I can live healthily and happily ever after with ALL my hair.

I live in fear. I am afraid that someone will notice something wrong and draw attention to me. Then I'll be ashamed and embarrassed. I worry about people sitting behind me, about the wind blowing, about maybe this being a progressive disease, and about not stopping at all someday. I am afraid that if I don't keep fighting, IT will win.

During the past six months, especially, I have been working on developing tangible weapons to use in this civil war within myself. They seem to be either generalized tension releasers or specific head "treatments."

The general activities include cutting down on caffeine intake and making a point of drinking decaffeinated tea and spring water. Just making the tea requires my patience—while it heats, steeps, and then cools enough to drink. Walking the dog is relaxing and often I take photographs while I'm out; I make various kinds of collages and abstracts. The key is to keep BOTH my hands and my mind occupied. Also it is still hard for me to accept the idea that I can be active without tension.

When the urge to pull is strong, it is like my head "needs something," some kind of stimulation or attention. I keep toothpicks handy at home and in the car so I can chew on them. I have sharp combs around so that I can gently scratch my head. I wear stretchy headbands at home to create a kind of opposing and neutralizing tension. I try to refrain from nail biting because when I give up and chew them severely, it becomes even harder to not pull my hair.

It seems like there is common ground among the biochemistry and thinking patterns of alcoholism, trichotillomania, nail biting, and obsessive-compulsive behavior in general. For example, when I wanted to recover from drinking, I was very worried about dying drunk. Now I am worried that I might get to the end of my life with less than a full head of hair.

My dream is to be free of symptoms for weeks and months at a time instead of a few days. I am going to keep working on progress, not perfection.

Anne
Small Town, Maine

MEG'S STORY

I knew by the time my son was two years old that he was different. For the 17 years that followed, my husband and I both abused him emotionally. We wanted so badly for him to be "normal." We abused him while loving him deeply.

At age 19 he became so obsessed with ritualistic praying and worrying that he was not saved, that I almost lost my mind. He was forced to drop out of college and was very depressed. A year later, while on Prozac, he began drinking, being even more depressed, and wanted to kill himself. The doctor hospitalized him while we awaited the approval of Anafranil for research (3 months). During that time his anxiety level increased by leaps and bounds.

As of April 1993 he has been on 250 mg. of Anafranil for four years. He works at a full time job, lives at home, and is happy with life. He seldom complains but still does not have the concentration or self discipline to go back to college. In general, he is doing great. He says he would "kill for his medication" because it makes the quality of life so much better.

We have had a very stormy life, but thanks to a great doctor, James Claghorn, and Anafranil, we are now surviving.

Meg
Texas

CATHERINE'S STORY

How does one begin to tell the story of one's decline into mental, emotional and spiritual darkness? Total blackness. Hell. From 1983 to 1991 I was there. I lived there, slept there, ate and drank there. I existed in total darkness. There were times that I felt I could hand on no longer. There were times when suicide seemed like the only possible answer. In fact, I took a handful of sleeping pills shortly after the onset of my OCD because I was so desperate for mental peace. To be able to stop thinking, even for a few minutes, seemed the ultimate gift. I didn't die and I am so glad. Even when I woke from my overdose, I was glad. But still, in reality, my battle with OCD was only in the very beginning stages. Hell was to last for seven more long years.

I have a type of Obsessive-Compulsive Disorder known as religious scrupulosity. Everything I was obsessed with in those eight years had to do with religion. I had always had a particularly close relationship with God; but one day my mind turned it into a relationship of punishment and fear, no longer one of joy and acceptance. I was a senior in college and I was sitting in one of my business classes. I had Dr. Smith (name has been changed), the toughest and most rude teacher I'd ever had. Dr. Smith singled me out in class one day. He was always digressing into some little story, and suddenly he turned to me and said, "Catherine, life's a bitch and then you die, isn't that right?" I said, "Uh, yes." I was so embarrassed; everyone was looking at me. I said, "Uh, yes." It was over. But something happened inside me. The thought came into my mind that what I had done, agreeing with Dr. Smith, was a horrible sin. "How could I do something like that? If God feels I look at life that way, He'll be mad at me. Until I somehow take back what I said, I'll be living in a constant state of sin. God will punish me morning, noon and night. Oh my goodness, I am a filthy, wretched person. I don't deserve God's love. I am so horrible, so sinful." By now my mind was racing a mile a minute. These thoughts turned into a sickening obsession. Hour after hour I was consumed with these thoughts. If someone spoke to me, I completely missed it because my mind was on a treadmill that only one act of mine could solve: Do something to take it back. To amend it. After a few minutes of my mind's racing over this issue, it came to me. Tomorrow was Valentine's Day. I would send Dr. Smith a Valentine card and I would write him a little message in it telling him that I didn't mean what I had said. So that is what I did. I put it in the mail and almost immediately the obsession went away. I was now on good terms with God again. He had reaccepted me into His fold. Needless to say, Dr. Smith looked at me sort of funny two days later; but even though I was embarrassed from thereon in his class for sending mean old Dr. Smith a Valentine's card with a ridiculous message inside, I was right with God again.

Obsessions such as the one mentioned above were a dime a dozen. I was constantly performing little acts or praying for hours on end to amend for some horrible evil I had done. Another good example was jogging. I loved it and I loved feeling in shape. It was one of the few things that I felt I did well and it meant a great deal to me. But one day, someone said something to me about how jogging stimulated the brain chemical endorphins (something that I already knew), and that you could become addicted to the high you feel after a good run. For the first time something clicked in my mind. I told myself, "If I jog, then the endorphins will become stimulated and they will take over my mind and then the devil will possess me because I will no longer have control." Every time I jogged I was not able to finish because this obsession would become so severe. The answer? I stopped jogging. I took up walking, but I even made myself walk slowly so as not to get those endorphins stimulated.

One of the worst obsessions? Anxiety itself (the obsession's best friend). I had a minister friend tell me once, in counselling, that the devil used anxiety as a tool against us. Well, anxiety was something I was experiencing almost 24 hours a day. Even when I could quench an obsession through ceaseless prayer or an act of some sort, there was always another obsession ready to pop out. I was rarely sleeping nights now. A doctor gave me sleeping pills (which is what I overdosed on). When the minister told me this, it threw me into such a horrible tailspin. That night was to be the worst night of my life. I lay in bed wide awake until it was time to get up the next morning, being obsessed about what he had told me. "I must live in a constant state of wickedness because I feel anxiety all day and night," I thought. But the harder I tried to get rid of the anxiety, the more severe it got. Thus, the feeling of being evil. No words put on paper could adequately describe the pain and torment that this obsession caused me. My mind went back and forth, back and forth. This obsession (probably the worst one I ever had) was not to last days, but years. Finally, through a loving, Christian husband, good therapists, and an ever-loving Lord, I was to work through this obsession and get it out of my system. But there were others. Always, always others.

I could go on and on and on, each obsession being different but with that same thread woven throughout each one: I was evil and wicked. Unless I beat myself day and night by imposing strict prayer demands upon myself, or unless I cleansed my life completely of all its enjoyments (for enjoyments must be wicked), then I was going to hell and that was all there was to it.

But it's over. In the spring of 1991, after the birth of a beautiful baby girl, I went on Anafranil. My life is forever changed. I jog, I feel anxious occasionally, I have a beer once in a while, I laugh at a colorful joke, etc., etc., etc. And you know something? God loves me so much! Why? Because Jesus Christ has always lived in my heart (as a little girl I asked Him to), and He never looked at me the way I feared He did. I could debate endlessly on the issues of why I suffered all those years. If God loved me so much, then why? This type of question every person must ponder in his or her own heart. But, deep in the depths of my heart, tucked away in some little corner, God told me to hang on because I was going to make it. My mom and dad always told me that I had this special determination about me. I guess they were right.

Catherine J.

Westfield, Massachusetts

Special love and thanks to: Brian, Mom and Dad, Jessica and Meg, and all my friends who were there for me.

RJW'S STORY
"Some Recalled OC Behaviors, Incidents, etc."

Fear of Personal Contamination/Harm

Fear of "The Blob" as seen in previews at movie theater, Bradford, Pennsylvania, December 1961, at age 10. I crawled over a bunch of friends to get reassurance from my father because I was struck by the terror of the possibility of the Blob's being real. I continued to be obsessed by the Blob for weeks after.

During the same period of my life I was caught playing in an open drainage ditch which contained sewage. In order to persuade me not to play in the ditch in the future, my father worked up a graphic and terrifying description of Typhoid Fever. I became convinced that I already had it and was terrified for days. When I was in the 4th or 5th grade I was playing with a friend who got carried away and sort of "drummed" on my head. A few days later I decided that there was something "wrong" with my head and became very fearful of imminent death. This incident was finally resolved when I went into the hospital for three days for X-rays and observation. There I acquired my first of a long line of professional reassurances and developed an awareness and appreciation of the value of good health.

During the years I used snuff chewing tobacco along with alcohol as medication. I became increasingly worried about oral cancer, as well I should have; but I was worried about it way before anyone knew about it—essentially I "made it up." I sought reassurance for years from doctors, dentists, etc. My addiction to tobacco in combination with this fear of cancer was particularly hellish. I entered into a period of extraordinary fear of AIDS (a disease that I had "created" long before its existence became known). Even talking about it was equivalent to getting it for me. Because I was sexually active with more than one partner during this time, I became increasingly afraid. I made up highly unlikely but possible scenarios of how I had contracted it. This caused me to avoid some people entirely and to avoid certain meetings.

Scrupulosity

I became obsessed with the perfect examination of conscience and confession. I had a standard list of sins which was often inflated just for good measure. I made up sins and confessed them just in case. I found it nearly impossible to live in a state of grace between the time of my confession and the time of receiving Holy Communion; in the Catholic Church this is the most unforgivable No-No which involves immediate and secret condemnation to hell. This was true even if the confession was made just before the Mass!

I would often not go to Communion—sometimes I was conspicuously the only person in a whole section of the church who would not go. I was often in a state of anguish. At its worst I had to be physically removed from a confessional because I kept going back and telling more and more.

In high school freshman year (1963-1964) I had a recurrence of scrupulosity which involved much of the same behavior experienced years earlier. I was wrestling that year and, in part, my wrestling was limited by my concern over the safety of my opponent! I took to carrying a rosary around in my pocket all the time that year, saying it constantly. I tried to make each prayer, each phrase of each "Hail Mary" perfect. I made up extra prayers to say on the chain links between the beads. I frequently had to start over and over and over, often falling asleep at night in total exhaustion.

In later years when I would be at some point of enjoyment, contentment or relaxation in my life, I would immediately turn to a vast examination of conscience, seeking things to worry about from the past. This spoiled many beautiful life experiences for me.

Body Dysmporphic Disorder

In the 7th and 8th grade I was considerably overweight. My nickname was "Fats." I didn't like it because I had come, during this time, to the awareness that I was a good-looking person. I was attracted to girls and wanted them to be attracted to me. So, in freshman year in high school I went out for wrestling as a way to lose weight. By a series of twists and turns I ended up wrestling varsity as a freshman and lettering. That entire season and for each season thereafter I was obsessed with my weight and what I ate. I used to ration even the amount of water that I drank. I was severely underweight by the end of the season but unwilling even to admit it.

In conjunction with the weight loss I arose every morning and did a regimen of squat-thrusts and sit-ups in my room prior to getting ready for school. I HAD to do these every morning and I HAD to do them more and better each day until they were really getting in the way of my, and others', morning life. My mother attempted to physically stop me at least once, but I persisted.

During my freshman-junior years at college (1970-72), I became concerned that I was freakishly short and misshapen. I bought and wore heavy hiking boots for years because the thick soles gave me more height. I made up a false name (Shorty Long!) and ordered body-stretching information through the mail. This affected my self image and social interactions for more than two years. After I decided that there was nothing that I could do about being freakishly short, I became convinced that I was losing my hair. I was constantly looking in the mirror at my hair line. I developed a variety of magic rituals of hair care (brushing, massaging, etc.) designed to prevent this. (Twenty years later my hairline is in the exact same place that it was then.)

After my freshman year at Pitt I was overweight again. I weighed 185. I became determined to lose weight and re-experienced behavior similar to my wrestling days plus genuine bulimia. I would eat and purge, then eat again. I became quite good at making myself gag.

Responsibility OC

It was in response to responsibility contamination fears that I first started excessive hand-washing. Rather than a fear of personal contamination, the hand-washing rituals were always centered on PREVENTION of my contaminating others. Related to the sexual contamination fears about the nature of my own sexual fluid were fears of contamination by urine and feces, both mine and others', as well as dog-do, etc. I got involved in terrifying rituals of wiping toilets and washing hands and wiping toilets and washing hands while getting completely wrapped in the mental snarl of "I'm contaminating, I'm getting contaminated."

The fear of contaminating others is one of my longest-lasting and most strongly ingrained rituals. To this day, it is difficult for me to grasp a doorknob or other door-opening device without going through a flash assessment of the "two-way contamination" scenario. I still have the urge to wipe doorknobs, as I have for years with my trusty friend the paper towels, but, in general, I resist. But I still find some very interesting ways to get through doors without actually grabbing the doorknob. This ritual also extends to numerous other publically-handled objects, such as diner salt and pepper shakers, chairs, money, etc. The urge to tell others was one of the ways that I alleviated the Responsibility OC fears. I would tell the person whom I had contaminated (usually getting some very strange and uncomfortable looks in return), or I would find someone to whom I could describe the entire event and be reassured.

Some of my most bizarre rituals involved the fear of setting or leaving "booby traps" for innocent people. This took many forms, but one which was with me for a long time was a concern over broken glass. If I broke a glass, it was a painful ritual to clean it up, fearing that if I left one sliver, it would be in some way fatal to someone. When I ran on the roads, if I saw glass, it became my responsibility to clean it up or move it. This was especially true if I touched it with my shoes, making it "mine." This fear took a bizarre form in the fall of 1991 before Prozac took effect. I had an old Ford pick-up truck which I had developed a fear about driving. It was very rusty and it flaked off rust all over the place when I closed the doors, etc. I became obsessed that the rust flakes would puncture a car tire. I avoided driving it, and the last time that I moved the truck I felt so uncomfortable that I had to go back over the route (at night with a flashlight) and look for rust.

Once I got it home I spent four hours under it scraping and brushing all the rust off and making sure that I bagged and discarded it.

The responsibility fear reached its zenith in my fear of killing someone via hit and run. At times (1976) I became so debilitated by this fear that I was unable to drive. My rituals related to this fear involved re-driving routes and constantly checking the rear-view mirrors. Sometimes, during the interval that it took to check the mirror, I'd imagine that I had hit someone else. I'd have to re-check the route, checking ditches for bodies. Once I actually made it to where I was going, I'd check over the vehicle for signs of impact, blood, etc. Finally, I would buy the newspapers and look for notices of hit and run accidents along my routes. I eventually purchased lots of mirrors for my truck. This helped, but then I was worried about hitting someone with these mirrors, which stuck out quite far. And on and on and on...

Hoarding

I have had mild hoarding symptoms all along. The most obvious form of this behavior is related to my collecting geological samples. I have been excessive in this regard since starting original research in 1975. Even when dredge hauls made during research cruises recovered tens of pounds of essentially the same stuff, I became reluctant to discard anything. As a result, I have one of the most extensive collections of carbonate rocks and sediment ever assembled from the Caribbean, but very little published on any of it. This behavior also extends to things such as pens and pencils and tools in general.

I have been OCD for over 30 years and have recently found an effective treatment in the form of medication (Prozac) and behavior modification therapy.

R.J.W.
Massachusetts

BARBARA'S STORY

Doctors—they don't see the despair, the torture, the dead eyes. I've only met two in my life who had an inkling that I was once a person and now I'm an OCD.

Doctors don't grasp the depth of hell, the nightmare, the war within ourselves just to live. They're in another world. The deep anger, the rage that comes from terrible anxiety and fear. What have doctors said to me, my nerves hanging from threads? "I can't work with you, you're too angry;" "your letters are so tragic, but you seem all right;" "oh, you are wearing a nice dress today, you must be feeling better."

Doctors—they only understand screaming and crying and tell you that you are better than others. They don't see that if you are missing a leg, it doesn't help to say someone is missing two. They act like it's a minor problem and you are weak, so weak. They add to the terrible guilt and shame that you already feel.

Anxiety grips me with such teeth; it is eating me alive like a carnivorous animal.

Years ago I could wash it away; the few moments that I felt it were bad moments to me. Now it is not moments but every second of every day, waiting for relief that you know never comes.

Another really bad day. What do you do when you feel so dirty and itchy? It's so horrible. All the things hanging up look so awful but I have to put them on; I have no choice. It's very bad. All day and night I think about them and what to do. Oh God, I waste my mind night and day just trying to survive. So afraid to touch things but being forced to. I can't explain it. It hurts so much. I feel so sick from it. So drained. It looks like I have so many clothes, but they are old and junky and I can't throw them away. The closets confuse me so. One is an open one and I knew that it would be a problem. It looks such a mess and the little one where I put my coats is such a problem. My bag of laundry goes in there and I worry that it dirties my coats and shoes; then it's hard to put them on. If I use the hamper it will dirty the bathroom. When I do the laundry, I carry 10 pounds just by the fingers of one hand, and it hurts so. I can't hold the bag against me or with two hands; I have to hold my coat with my other hand so it doesn't touch the laundry; and I have to wear a certain coat on these days, and a thousand other rituals. I've ruined my hands and fingers.

My dresser—drawers filled with junk and having to stuff things into the few drawers that I can use. I can't make up my mind to throw away anything, so it just accumulates and accumulates and there is no room for anything, and I don't know where anything is. I can't keep things neat and folded, I just have to throw everything inside quickly.

Why is it even harder to breathe now? Why this terrible feeling of everything being so dirty, even the "clean" clothes on my back? There is no answer, for the human mind and heart are made up of millions of emotions and happenings much more complex than any computer or doctor can analyze completely. I have an iron will to keep going in spite of terrible suffering. My possessions are such a mess, such confusion. All remnants of nothingness. There is no sense, no order. I have lost control. I feel that it is nearing completeness, and no one cares; and, if they see, they surely do not care to mention it or just do not know how to help. My so-called close friends don't want to hear a word of anything sad, and this is way beyond sad. I am very alone. I never thought that my days would be spent lying in bed endlessly—evenings, weekends, holidays, so very alone. On those rare occasions that I do go out for a little while, it is so uncomfortable that I want to get back. I am so trapped.

I drag my mnd for the memories of the free person that I once was—just to walk in the air and feel alive. I have to lie here and feel afraid, encircled by a bed, a room, my life. So trapped, so filled with self-hatred and anxiety that never stops even in my dreams or sleep. Up most of the night, thinking of my bed and my sheets and wondering, wondering, why can't I ever feel clean or free, free enough to even put on a nice, clean dress and walk down the street?

I just dress to cover my naked body; there is NO CHOICE. I am uncomfortable and ashamed always. I just have to bear it.

Barbara A.
New York, New York

DAVID'S STORY

I am a 51-year-old male named Dave with a lovely wife and three girls. In October of 1992 I was diagnosed as having severe OCD. Now that I look back at my life, I can see that I had symptoms of OCD as a teenager, but went undiagnosed. A lot of the problems that resurfaced were problems I can relate to in my earlier age. I was 19 years old when I can remember that I was constantly checking things. Some of the things I would check would be the oil dipstick on the car and the tires to see if they were low. I not only checked the tires and oil, but was very uncomfortable unless I checked them four times. This number doesn't mean anything to me, but subconsciously it must have some bearing, because it comes back to me in later life.

At the age of 27 I got married and noticed that I was saying and doing things repetitively. Also, as a child, and up until six months ago, I had severe tics, such as coughing, mouth twitching, clearing my throat, etc. During the first year of my marriage, I noticed that I was constantly asking my wife things that now don't seem to make much sense. But at that time, I would ask for reassurance. I also would ask the same question four times, and it had to be in four different rooms of a small, five-room house. I would ask my wife for an answer to a question or something that I did that I thought wasn't correct. As part of the ritual, I would repeatedly ask her if she were sure in one room, then corner her in another room, and ask her if she were positive. Then, a third time I would ask her if she were double sure, and a fourth time if she were double positive (whatever that meant). I would not feel comfortable unless I heard the answer four different times. The problem now became that one question led to a series of questions. My wife would run out of the house and I would chase her, asking questions. It was a scary time for her, as we had dated for five years prior to our marriage, and somehow I was able to hide these symptoms. Somehow, I started getting over it and went into a slight remission. One thing led to another, and a few years later I sunk into a deep depression with severe withdrawal from the community and high anxiety. (I would have to fight to stay at work because I had a feeling that I would want to "run out" of work.) I was constantly coming home from work, not eating supper, crying, and going to bed at six o'clock at night until six in the morning, leaving my wife to raise three young children. The only thing that kept me going was having an understanding wife, and constantly looking at the picture of my three girls on my desk at work. I had the feeling that I was constantly shaking and afraid to answer the telephone. I had a nervous stomach and also felt that I could cry at a moment's notice. To me, the pain that I felt was more severe than the pain of cancer. I think that I could have taken physical pain much better than mental pain.

One night my wife suggested to me that I meet with a young psychiatrist who was just starting to practice. This was around 1980. I saw him and he started me on multiple medications, including Imipramine and Xanax. The Imipramine caused me to gain a lot of weight, but after three months of medication, I began to feel better and went into a remission for quite a few years. In 1990, my mother died quite unexpectedly, and I began to notice that I was acting strangely, with repetitive questions coming back, and always feeling that I was saying the wrong thing to people. I began to ask my wife for reassurance and, although I did not ask her in different rooms, I did ask her four times, seeking reassurance that I had not said or done anything wrong.

I also began with a symptom of checking. I would return home from work and wonder if I had left the air conditioner on or hadn't locked the doors to the office. I already had checked these items several times before leaving work. In order to rest the situation in my mind, I would drive back to work (a half hour ride each way) to recheck the door and air conditioner. Every time I went back, everything was closed and locked properly. On one occasion, I nearly missed a flight that my wife and I were taking to Las Vegas because I knew I would be out of work for several days, felt uncomfortable, started home, then went back to work twice. Both times I was nearly half way home.

These rituals continued to happen and I noticed that I was checking more and more things than I had been, many times in multiples of four. On one occasion, I went from the upper level of the house to the den in the basement to check the meaning of a word in the dictionary at least four times. One word led to another and another, and I continued to go up and down the stairs numerous times. My wife got quite disturbed, as she knew something was wrong.

The problem also magnified itself at work. I was constantly checking the input data I put into the computer many, many times. I would also check the folders in the filing cabinets many times. It became increasingly difficult to resist these temptations, and I noticed that I was picking up more symptoms.

The day I bottomed out was when I went to my psychiatrist, in October of 1992, and he told me he didn't know what to do to help me, and that, because I was having a difficult, if not impossible, time at work, that he would get me permanent disability. I never lost the will to get better. I came home and told my wife, and both of us had a good cry. It was at this point that my life began to turn around.

That night I called Butler Hospital in Rhode Island and told the woman the symptoms that I had and asked her in desperation if there was anyone on their staff who could help me. I explained to her my symptoms, and she put me in contact with Dr. Steve Rasmussen. I saw him several times and he started me on a new medication. The doctor went out of his way to see me on a Sunday morning. He also put me in contact with an OCD therapist, Barbara Vannoppen. My wife and I began to see Barbara once a week, and she would explain what this illness was, and gave me strategies and challenges to use. After a while, I noticed that I was improving and had to go to the therapist less often. I also began going to some of these sessions alone. Along with this, I attended a monthly group meeting on OCD and did group behavioral therapy with 13 people. At one point I had gone to the hospital four times in a week between therapy and doctors' visits. My will to overcome this dreadful disease was becoming more powerful. I had been on a high level of Xanax (8 mg.) from a previous physician. Dr. Rasmussen began to get me off the medication. It was very difficult, as I had severe withdrawal symptoms. All of this was going on as I continued to work and lead a somewhat secret life. I am now happy to say that in May of 1993, I am down to half a milligram of Xanax and will be completely off this medication in two months.

I am currently on Prozac, Buspar and Haldol (for multiple tics), continuing to see the doctor and also getting therapy, but not quite as often. I am now convinced that I will overcome this illness, but that every day will become a challenge. Almost every day OCD wants to act up. I have told myself that I must continue to fight and I will not let OCD win this battle.

David P.
Cranston, Rhode Island

JANE'S STORY

OCD started with me at a later age than with most people. The onset of my symptoms started at the age of 27. I had a very gradual progression into the illness. By the time I was 31, I finally sought help from a psychiatrist. This was when I was actually diagnosed with OCD. At that time, 1981, medication was not available, or behavior therapy either. I continued to have several years of psychotherapy, grew more comfortable with my OCD, and finally stopped my therapy.

In 1989, my son was in a devastating and deadly tornado. Twenty-one people were killed and several hundred were injured. Hours passed and we couldn't find him. I feared that we would never see him alive. Finally, he was found in a hospital, injured but alive.

Within the next week, my OCD symptoms reached their highest peak. I was at my worst. After this, I realized that extremely stressful and tragic events triggered OCD. After the tornado, I was so taken with my obsessions and compulsions that I couldn't leave my house. Contamination was everywhere, so I washed and cleaned from waking until going to sleep. It was then that I wrote the poem that follows.

I was desperate for help. I went back to my former psychiatrist and when I got an appointment with him, he prescribed Prozac for me.

Within several weeks, I felt that I was more in control. What a relief! After a few months, I decided to try behavior therapy. The psychologist was well-educated in behavior therapy for OCD, and he helped to guide me in my progress. I'm very grateful to both doctors for their help.

I gradually grew more confident, and with the help of a local psychiatrist, started a support group in Huntsville. I feel it's been very successful and the number of members in our group has grown. We have a special closeness and understanding of each other.

The treatment for OCD has come a long way. You're not alone in this long and painful chain of rituals and thoughts. Right now I'm very functional and happy. You can be, too! Hang in there and know that you will see better days.

THOUGHTS OF AN OCD PATIENT

I wish that I were normal.
I feel so all alone.
It seems that others look at me
As if I wasn't whole.

Some people think I'm crazy.
I just wish they'd understand.
They say, "why don't you stop it?"
It makes me feel real bad.

I spend my days washing,
Till my hands are chapped and rough.
I can't seem to do much else.
It makes my life real tough.

Germs are unseen enemies
That torture me each day.
I wonder what would happen
If I didn't wash these things away.

I can't seem to control
What's going on inside my head.
I wish that I could stop it,
But I wash and wash instead.

It's hard for my family to endure this.
They aren't used to my strange ways.
Sometimes they lose their patience,
As we live through these long days.

These rituals that go on each day
Make our lives a living hell.
I pray that someday very soon
I'll be completely well.

In order to get through this
You must talk these thoughts away.
Try very hard not to give up,
Struggling day by endless day.

I sympathize with the people
That suffer as I do.
I wish for them all to know,
I know what they're going through.

Jane
Huntsville, Alabama

ROB'S STORY

NAME: ROB
DOB: 11/18/67
ILLNESS: OCD with self-mutilation—15½ years; alcoholism, drug addiction—13 years.
HOSPITALIZATIONS: 10 (4 suicide attempts)
MEDICATIONS: Present: Anafranil, Sinequan, Buspar
                    Past: Triavil, Lithium, Klonopin, Trilafon, Haldol,
                    Mellavil, Xanax, Librium, Vistaril, Ativan, Antabuse,
                    Cogentin
MISDIAGNOSIS: Learning disability; Depressive with obsessive tendencies

As you can see from the above, my OCD experience really started when I was 10 years old. Since it started in 1978 I can honestly say that there has not been a single day in which I have had absolutely no symptoms at all. This disease, like many other types of mental illness, can be relentless in its attacks. However, it can be dealt with through medicine and therapy and if you set realistic goals you more than likely will achieve them. One advantage that there is to having OCD as opposed to other types of mental illness is that, unlike many of the others, we do not lose touch with reality. We don't believe the insanity that our illness causes us to think. Also, we do not alway appear to be ill, often due to our diligent efforts to hide our illness from others (an aspect that at times hurts us more than it helps us).

But my intent in writing this letter is not to talk about all the aspects of our illness. Instead, it is to warn you off the idea that drugs or alcohol will offer you an escape from your illness, because they will not. At the very most they may make you temporarily indifferent to the symptoms that are plaguing you. This brief indifference, on the other hand, is always followed by a blitzkrieg of symptoms.

Quite simply, what I am saying is that drugs and alcohol will really do nothing more than amplify your symptoms and increase your torment. It has taken me 13 years and eight of my nine lives to realize that this idea is indeed true. My biggest regret to this day is that I made my symptoms worse with drugs and alcohol. I increased my suffering, suffering that I could have avoided by simply stopping what I was doing, a luxury that I was not afforded in my acquisition of OCD.

Don't confuse your brain chemistry any more than it is. Don't use drugs or alcohol. Don't suffer more than you have to.

Rob F.
Hackensack, New Jersey

Patience is the blood of victory
Faith is her soul
Courage is her body
Noble are her goals

Rob F.

TRUDY'S STORY

Trudy B. called me this morning from West Virginia. She had read about this book in the OC Foundation's newsletter, and she wanted very much to be able to contribute some of her story for it. But Trudy had a small problem. As badly as she wanted to put something down on paper for this project, she was unable to do so because of a severe checking compulsion. At this time, Trudy's brain will not allow her to simply sit down, tear off a few pages, and mail it out. So this is the only time that I have interviewed anyone for this book. Trudy, I certainly hope that I do you the justice that you deserve, for you are definitely, as Louis L'Amour wrote, "A woman to ride the river with."

At 36 years of age, Trudy has been experiencing OCD in some very severe forms for the last 20 years, give or take a year or two. From the time that she was a young girl, Trudy knew that she was "different," but she didn't know why or just how much, as she never had anyone to talk with about the things that she did. As she puts it, she has spent her entire life hiding, feeling like a secret agent.

In March of '87, Trudy was watching 20/20 when they aired their program on OCD. BINGO! She suddenly knew what her life was all about. It took her two more years to gather the courage to try to seek some kind of professional help. There is no doubt that Trudy's perseverance is a testimony to her guts, as she went from a psychiatrist to a psychologist to a therapist to yet another psychiatrist, until she was finally able to find someone who didn't fall asleep while she was talking, who didn't tell her abruptly to "just stop it!", and who had somewhat of a clue as to just what Obsessive-Compulsive Disorder is all about. Consequently, Trudy was able to take part in one of the Anafranil trials in this country, and she does find that she has some success with this medication.

"Some success" does not mean that Trudy is cured. She has a plethora of obsessions and compulsions, each overlapping the other, so that, as she puts it, "OCD is my career now." Trudy and her husband own a small business where she was an active partner in both the store and in doing the bookkeeping. That is, until one day when her brain said, "What we need here are fives in everything." So much for the bookkeeping for the moment. Trudy finds that her strongest, but certainly not her only, compulsions are checking, hoarding, praying, and counting. Some days there are certain rituals that are stronger and more intense than the others, but this is always subject to change.

As you can well imagine, Trudy's life is almost entirely taken up with this disease. She is engulfed by it every single day. With all this frustration and pain that she has, when I asked her, "What is it that gets you through the day?", Trudy's answer was very quick—her husband. She feels that, as her husband is a veteran of two tours of duty in Vietnam, he is a bit more sensitive to someone else's needs and pains.

Trudy told me that our conversation marked the very first time that she had ever talked with another person with OCD. I hope that this book makes it possible for Trudy to finally be able to speak with many others, openly, about this disease. I hope that Trudy is able, at last, to meet others like herself, who still have their dignity intact and are, like her, tired of a lifetime of acting. Over 20 years is an awfully long time to go along thinking that you're all alone in what you do. I'm proud of you, Trudy; thanks for calling.

Trudy B.
West Virginia

DARREN'S STORY

What can I tell you about Obsessive-Compulsive Disorder? Let me see. Well, the earliest manifestations of OCD that I can remember happened when I was nine or ten years old. Suddenly I began to wash my hands, again and again, never fully satisfied that they were clean. Logically, I knew that my hands weren't dirty, but there was this INTENSE FEELING THAT I JUST HAD TO WASH MY HANDS. If I didn't, I would be overcome by waves of anxiety. The only relief came when I surrendered and washed my hands, over and over again.

This was the beginning of 20 years spent dealing with OCD. I have lived through many different symptoms of this disorder—a veritable smorgasbord of washing, cleaning, checking, counting, and constant doubt.

I always thought that my obsessions and compulsions were the result of some character fault. No one had ever heard of OCD. What would today be easily recognized as classic signs of the illness were overlooked by family, teachers and professionals. I'm not angry at them; after all, very few people knew about OCD then. Not until 1988 did I first read about OCD in a newspaper article. Talk about a revelation! The story could have been written about me. As I read on, I came to the realization that I was not crazy. This behavior had a CHEMICAL origin. I was not to blame for all of my obsessions and compulsions. Most importantly, I now had a name for my illness. This would be the commencement of an ongoing battle with OCD and its consequences.

When you have OCD, it is likely that you will have other accompanying problems. Throughout my childhood and up to the present, I have always felt isolated, lonely and different. Anxiety and generalized fear are daily companions. I am constantly trying to escape from the seclusion of OCD.

People who know me may be surprised to learn that I have a mental illness. What must be understood about OCD is its secretiveness. I find the behavior repugnant and try my best to hide it. Sufferers of this disorder are marvelous actors and actresses, rivaling the best work of Brando or Hepburn. Somehow, we manage to cope and survive. Through a huge effort we continue to live and work as normally as possible. OCD drains your mental and physical energy. Overcoming the urge to perform some behavior is nearly impossible. Even when you aren't involved in a ritual or obsession, the specter of OCD looms large in your mind. It is a 24-hour-a-day struggle—even my dreams are vulnerable. It is hard not to hate oneself. OCD destroys your self-esteem.

People with OCD are survivors. For whatever reason, we have this illness to deal with. Life is all about challenges and obstacles. Obsessive-Compulsive Disorder is one great hurdle, but it can be fought. For some, medication may work. I've had only limited success with medicines such as Prozac, Anafranil and Zoloft. At best, they have alleviated the depression that comes with OCD. Behavior therapy may also help in some cases. Unfortunately, the availablitiy and quality of treatment for this disorder vary.

What have I found to be the best approach to OCD? It is a combination of support and education. With help from family and friends, and with good counseling, the isolation can be lifted. Teachers, professionals, and society should be informed about OCD, its effects, and how to recognize it. The years of suffering in silence are over. No one needs to wait years for treatment any longer.

I hope that, through continued research, a cure for OCD will be found. Until that time arrives, what I ask for is patience and understanding. Please know that I am trying my best to grapple with this illness. Pity or sympathy is not what I want. Rather, I would ask for words of encouragement and support. You can't imagine the mental pain that OCD inflicts upon its victims. Only a fellow sufferer can tryly understand the torture.

Whether you are a counter, a checker, a cleaner, or any other OCD subtype, you are not alone. It's not your fault. There is hope. Behind each child or adult with OCD there is a wonderful, unique person trying to break out and break free. Learn where the illness ends and the individual begins.

No one ever said life would be boring!

Darren F.
New York

JUDY'S STORY

OCD—this is one of the most, if not *the* most, difficult things I've had to deal with, although I truly do believe that LOVE conquers all! I don't mean that in an unrealistic way. Dealing with this illness is most difficult for the sufferer, and for the spouse, I feel that it is almost twice as difficult, because as we know, there is nothing worse than watching someone you love so much, hurt so bad. It takes love, patience, compassion, understanding, and last, but definitely not least, HUMOR!

When my husband is having an extremely bad time and he is screaming at me because he is so frustrated and he can't stand himself, and I'm so upset because it's not my fault, yet I become the SPONGE and absorb it all—I've actually bitten my hand as hard as I could without breaking the skin to release some of the tension and rage that I feel myself, so as not to yell back. Things have gotten so crazy that I just can't wait until he goes to sleep so I can have some sane and comforting time alone. After I've fallen asleep, sometimes I wake up an hour later shaking inside because of what I've gone through a few hours before; I've actually sucked my thumb to fall asleep (don't laugh—it worked!). I cry a lot, too, and that always makes me feel better!

We've been married for four years and we've had a lot of GREAT times and we've been to HELL and back—and I wouldn't give up a minute of it. Without the hard times, how can you truly appreciate the good ones?

I sound like I'm handling this all alone, and that's not true. My family, close friends and co-workers have been very supportive of me. But it's very difficult because so few people really know and fully understand OCD (nor do they want to).

I hate OCD so much because it robs me of my husband at times. When I'm upset or just want to talk, or need a hug, I want my husband. Well, that's just not possible sometimes. But when he is doing well, I get all the hugs that I can take! He is great most of the time except for a flare-up once in a while. OCD comes in peaks and valleys.

One minute, one hour, one day at a time is how I've learned to live, and that's not such a bad idea.

Never lose hope; they will find a cure—some minute, some hour SOMEDAY!

Judy

New Jersey

Author's Note: Judy is actually grappling with two diseases daily—her husband's OCD as well as her own MS.

JANIS' STORY

Those who are reading this book are probably either suffers of Obsessive-Compulsive Disorder (OCD), loved ones of a person afflicted with this illness (and I do believe it is an illness), or possibly health care professionals who are trying to learn more about OCD. I firmly believe that the best way to learn about any kind of illness is to go firsthand to those who suffer from it; to obtain their true feeling and opinions is the only real way to understand any illness. If someone has cancer, he would learn more about what treatment and recovery would be like from fellow cancer sufferers than from the doctors and other health care workers who have not personally experienced the affliction. I once joked, during my pregnancy, to my male obstetrician concerning my aches and pains, "How many babies have you had, to tell me how I should and do feel?" This is why I think this book is so important. It allows those of us who have OCD to not be alone. OCD can be a lonely illness.

I can not speak for all others with OCD as I had never spoken to anyone else with it until the other day, but I can give you my experienced opinion. To understand that, I will tell you a little bit about myself. I have been married to a very wonderful, supportive man for almost nine years. He is a high school teacher of whom I am very proud. We have a beautiful, talented three-year-old daughter. We own a small home in a suburb of a large, southern city. I am a housewife now. It sounds as though we have a white picket fence. The truth is that I have spent much of my days performing rituals/compulsions in an attempt to ease the extreme anxiety that accompanies my many obsessive thoughts.

The truth is that I used to be an accountant for a large teaching hospital until I had to quit. My compulsions were keeping me from performing my job. I was so tired all day long and could not sleep at night. I spent a majority of those sleepless nights also performing rituals. The obsessive thoughts became stronger and the compulsions increased. I was afraid to get out of bed. I could not take it any more. The question then comes to mind, "How and why did this behavior begin?" I had started to exhibit tendencies of OCD as a teenager. This subsided (I do not know why), and I suffered from small bouts of depression and OCD throughout college and employment. I graduated from college Magna Cum Laude with a Bachelor of Science in Business Administration and earned several promotions at my employment.

I became pregnant when I was twenty-six and my beautiful daughter was born. My pregnancy was very high-risk and I was on bed rest for four of the months of which I carried my daughter. I had her at eight months and she was born very ill and almost died. She, thank God, recovered. The doctors, though, seemed to want a reason for her illness. Everything always returned to me. What had I done wrong? Did I eat this or do that? Of course I already blamed myself and this fed this fear. Ironically, I had "compulsively" followed every pregnancy guideline. On top of this, when my daughter finally came home from the hospital, the doctors told us that a cold might kill her so we went out of our way to ensure her safety. I became the master of this. As a teenager, I had been through a similar experience with my mother. She had cancer and her immune system had been destroyed. I was reliving a nightmare.

As the months passed, my daughter became stronger, but my fears remained. I became obsessed with her becoming ill with a cold or anything else for that matter. It was unbearable. I felt as though I had to keep her from harm as I had been convinced that I had to have been the cause of all her problems from the start (even though intellectually I knew this was not true).

My obsessions soon began to grow. My two areas became germs and trust. I was so afraid of illness. When I returned to work after my daughter recovered, I caught the dreaded cold within a week. I can still hear my mother saying, "You brought it home to her." I do not even remember if she caught it, but I was not about to let myself hurt my daughter. I washed my hands as many as fifty times an hour. I wore a surgical mask to cover my face. I sterilized everything I touched. When I got better, I was petrified of catching another cold. I began having trouble at work. I got very anxious at meetings as someone always seemed ill. I began washing my telephone with alcohol several times a day to kill germs. It eventually got so bad that if someone seemed ill or had an ill relative, I could not touch a piece of paper that he had touched without being paralyzed with fear of germs. I would scrub my hands every time I got the mail. I could not touch the doorknob of the office. I began washing and scrubbing my hands more and more, even with cleanser. My hands cracked, bled and became infected. My productivity declined as I spent so much time washing my hands. As I stated earlier, I worked in a hospital and I had to walk its halls. This became impossible. I was afraid to breathe. I would carry paper towels to open doors. I could not ride an elevator and always had to walk the stairs. This soon transferred to other aspects of my life. I stopped wanting to see friends as they might have been ill. I did not want my daughter to visit any other children. I checked all people that I saw to see if their noses were running. If they coughed, I ran. I could not touch money or eat at a salad bar because both were contaminated. I began having to shower upon returning home from anywhere. I scrubbed everything at home with Lysol. I even began washing my hands with Clorox. I also brushed my teeth around 20 times a day as I felt that my mouth was contaminated.

I firmly believe that an obsession other than germs is involved in the compulsive washing. It is, for me, wanting to "wash" away my anger and frustration. This negativity is turned, of course, at myself. The more I get angry at myself, the more I punish myself and, no matter how much I wash, the frustration returns and then I wash more—an endless cycle.

The other area that seems to have been manifest for me is trust. Before my daughter's illness, I did not believe strongly in myself or my abilities, but afterward I did not think I could do anything right. Even though intellectually I knew that I had not caused her illness, emotionally I blamed myself. I had not been in contact with many children and I was not certain of my motherly instincts from the start. Now I believed, "If I ruined my pregnancy, what else will I do to my daughter?" I would boil her bottles again and again, not believing I had done it or well enough. I washed her clothing several times, not believing I had put soap in the washing machine. I checked my medication time and time again to ensure that it was out of her reach. The list is endless.

Like the washing, this transferred to other areas of my life. At work I did many reports which involved intricate numbers. I would check the figures an endless number of times. I was obsessed with the fear of making a mistake. Although I was quite accurate, my productivity declined even further. I constantly checked my keys to ensure that they were not lost. I checked my charge cards in my wallet to be certain that I had not lost them. I began taking vitamins and did not believe that I took them. I would take them again and again and eventually became very ill. Once again the effects were innumerable.

I finally became so consumed that 80% of my day was filled with compulsions to try to thwart my obsessions. It came to a head, so to speak, and I collapsed at work. Soon after that I had to quit my job. That has been hard on everyone and caused a major adjustment in finances. I wonder if I will ever be able to work again and I get angry at myself for this, as I believe, failure.

My illness, I feel, has been hard on everyone around me. In this, I must include myself. As a perfectionist, it is hard for me not to be "supermom." I felt that I should work an 80-hour week, keep the house spotless, and spend another 10 hours a day with my daughter in true quality time. On top of this, I have to have time for my obsessions and compulsions. I would probably have to have an 80-hour day. Of course, intellectually, I know all of the above is not possible, but emotionally I think it SHOULD be. It is also hard for me to intellectually accept OCD as an illness. I have a history of mental illness in my family and I was always told that those who have it should just be stronger and take charge of their lives. Those who have mental illness could just "stop it" if they wanted to do so. All of those "shoulds" become ingrained in a person's being. I have to accept OCD as an illness. This, in and of itself, has been hard and I admit that there are days that

I still awaken angry at myself for my problems.

My husband has been terrific. I often wonder why he has not just left me. I ask him why he stays and he tells me he loves me. I often do not believe him when he says this. I think that is just another factor of OCD.

I do believe that my husband becomes frustrated with me at times. I can not blame him. If someone does not have the thought pattern of a person with OCD, it must be hard to understand from where the compulsive behavior stems. It must be even harder for others with whom an OCD sufferer comes in contact. I am certain that those in my former workplace must have noticed that something was different about my behavior. As with any other major illness, though, acute OCD behavior can prove who really cares. That has been hard, but sometimes interesting for me. My parents, although they are extremely supportive and helpful, I can tell do not understand. They have encountered so many problems in their lives that I try not to exhibit many OCD symptoms when I am with them. This holds true of most people. I act as though I do not have OCD and I do not perform the compulsions as much as possible in public. This is very hard for me as the obsessive thoughts build and my anxiety level increases so much that I feel I might explode! I suppose I fear the reaction of others to my illness. Most of those with whom I have shared my illness have been anything but supportive. My brother and his wife treat me as though I am less of a person and they do not fully know from what I suffer. I can only imagine what they have told others as I have had virtual strangers approach me at mutual social functions concerned about my level of anxiety. My best friend from college was the first person (other than my husband) with whom I shared my OCD. She did not speak to me for a long time. She does not discuss it with me now; for her, it does not exist. Seeing these reactions (that hurt and actually feed the OCD with self-hate and that makes it worse) can make a person want to hide this illness even more.

My final thought is, "How do those of us with this affliction become better?" My answer is "I wish I knew." I can only tell you what I am doing and am going to do for myself. This is probably the key—doing for myself. I do not accept myself or like myself and I must learn to do so to recover. Just as the first step in an alcoholic's recovery, I believe, I had to admit that I have OCD to become any better. It helps to surround oneself with people who accept you as you are—OCD included. As I stated earlier, this is not easy. For me, I must thank my husband, my true best friend, and my cousin. With them I can be myself and they love and accept me. I must also acknowledge the support of my parents, my aunt, and my uncle. I am in therapy for the depression that accompanies the OCD. My husband goes with me whenever I want him to do so. My therapist, though, does not address my OCD very often. I believe I will have to find my own solution. She has told me, though, that I will never be perfect (as I feel my emotions should be like those of a robot). I take Zoloft which is helping to take the edge from the anxiety. This drug is beginning to become more common in treating OCD (I took Anafranil but could not tolerate the side effects). I do not believe in behavior modification as I have tried this and relaxation techniques and they help on a short-term basis, but my underlying obsessions are still present and eventually the overwhelming anxiety causes me to perform the compulsions—often, more than I had previously. I think, for me, I must first learn to accept myself as me and as human, but not perfect. This is harder that it sounds. I think to do this I must listen to those who accept me with OCD. While this may be just a few people, they love me no matter what. I am also going to begin to search for others like myself, who suffer in silence. I think that support groups can do great things as more insight into how others feel helps us to understand ourselves. I must also stop trying to put myself on a timeline for recovery. This is not feasible. I found, after my daughter's illness, that helping others who had similar problems, by talking and comforting, helped me to better cope with my feelings. I believe that this also holds true for OCD. All of us who suffer form this illness must band together for better awareness of this affliction. The media must become more aware of it for more research to be done for a true cure and to gain society's acceptance. This will require more of us to lose our anonymity with this illness which is often a large part of our daily lives—suffering in silence. For me, I will begin speaking out about my illness and will try to research and write more about it (I have always wanted to be a writer). We must be brave, accept, learn, and support one another with OCD. We are human, we are not crazy, and we are not alone. We must help each other and accept ourselves—A TALL ORDER!

Janis
Jacksonville, Florida

MONICA

Our daughter Monica committed suicide in 1989 at the age of 25 years after years of living with OCD. For the last few years it completely controlled her life. She had other, probably related, problems: she was minimally brain damaged; severely depressed and anxious; and an alcoholic with a life-style that did much to complicate her already complex problems.

There's no way to know what combination of problems led to her suicide, but we believe that a huge contributing factor was the birth of a baby five or six weeks before her death, whom she had wanted adopted, but for whom she was declared incompetent to decide. Consequently, she was trying to deal with the father's wish to keep the baby, in the face of her obsessive fear of harming the baby, not directly but through her thoughts. Her decision to kill herself might well have been her choice of the lesser of two evils.

In the last few months of her life she was, she told me, never without obsessive thoughts, which she could not tell me about but which she was sure could hurt other people and had done so. (In retrospect, remembering certain of her comments and behavior over the years, we believe she felt responsible for the deaths of several family members and friends.) She frequently hung up on me in the middle of a phone conversation, sure that her thoughts would harm me.

Besides having obsessive thoughts, she was compulsive about many ordinary daily routines, most overwhelmingly, hygiene and grooming. She swung from the extreme of staying in the shower or washing her hands for hours to not showering or washing at all, sometimes for weeks, because she knew that once she started, stopping would be too difficult and painful. Her beautiful deep red hair was a curse to her because she could never arrange it exactly as she wanted it, and would spend hours trying, especially if she had to go someplace. She was always late, and many times completely failed to get places, especially medical and dental appointments, of which she was terribly fearful, but even places that she wanted to go. Should she avoid cleaning up in an effort to get someplace, the hair routines would take over and keep her from getting out of the bathroom.

She was also terrified of having her hair touched by anything that might "pollute" it. Preparing food and eating were thus causes for anxiety, as was taking any liquid medications or using lotions or creams anywhere on her body because they might get from her hands or mouth or face onto her hair. She flinched away from the touch of children (though she had always loved and been loved by them) and from the hugs and kisses of family members. She needed constant reassurance that nothing in her vicinity that could contaminate her hair had touched it. However, no amount of reassurance was ever enough to convince her. She had to change her sheets and pillowcase whenever she thought they might be dirty, at her worst times several times a day, the pillowcase most often because it inevitably touched her hair.

Monica had other compulsive rituals that contributed to her life's being taken over by OCD. She could smoke a cigarette only if she put it in the exact middle of her mouth. Failing that, she threw it away and started again, using as many cigarettes as it took to get one placed correctly.

She had to open and close doors and drawers in a certain way, and continued opening and closing until she got it right.

She had to walk in the middle of the sidewalk and would either shove people aside who got in her way or retreat to the side and wait until her path was clear before continuing down the middle.

Although she was an imaginative writer from childhood, she finally completely gave up writing —whether letters, reminder lists, stories or poetry—because she got to the point where she crossed out more words than not, because they were wrong in some way. This compulsion got so strong that she had to start on a new page after the first cross-out. In her belongings we found hundreds of pages with only two or three words written on them, the last one or two crossed out.

There were, undoubtedly, other compulsions that I've forgotten or that she didn't tell me about or that I didn't observe. But there's no question that her compulsive rituals and obsessive thoughts finally preoccupied her almost totally.

I wish I could say that the disease wasn't Monica, that she was able to function and have a life in spite of it, but I can't. I wish I could say that she became what she gave promise of being in her early years. She was joyous and loving, witty, sensitive to others, very bright in anything to do with language, a lover of music and reading (especially poetry and drama), an avid camper, a sought-after baby-sitter, a teller of stories and a writer, and an animal lover (but at the same time the only one of three sisters with the courage to kill spiders, for which job she was often called upon to perform by her much older but much more squeamish sisters). She was, simply, a joy to her family—grandparents as well as sisters and parents. We all called her special long before we heard the term "special child" as a euphemism for mentally disabled.

But OCD gradually took over and pushed into the background or destroyed almost all of Monica's special qualities. Watching that process without being able to do anything about it was so painful that it is still hard for me to say which constituted the worst tragedy, her life or her suicide.

Her personality changed completely. She became increasingly sullen and withdrawn, hostile and paranoid. She came to the point where she couldn't take care of herself or her animals. She couldn't finish even one semester of college, though she started many times. She never held a job, except for a few weeks as a companion to an elderly couple and a very short stint as a live-in baby-sitter; from both situations she was fired. She couldn't pursue any of her interests. She couldn't live at home both because she wanted to be independent of her parents and because of the toll her problems took on us mentally and physically. Most devastating of all, she couldn't get any real help. Finally, alcohol became her anesthetic and also helped her destroy herself.

I wish I could take the comfort that is intended in all the "you did all you could" comments that have been made to us. But I feel like a failure, I feel guilty, and I feel overwhelmingly sad at our loss and at Monica's many losses.

It's true that we did try to help in many ways and for many years, but that fact would bring us real comfort only if we had succeeded in any of our efforts. But we just didn't have any good information about OCD or any access to professionals who had experience treating it until so late in Monica's life that there were too many other complications: her alcoholism; the emotional problems developed over all those terrible years; and, not least of all, her complete distrust of any kind of intervention as a result of experience after experience over a period of twelve years of inept or downright harmful therapy.

Ironically and sadly, Monica killed herself on the morning of an appointment that she considered her last chance—an appointment to assess her eligibility for in-patient treatment in a newly opened OCD center, the first in our area.

Mary Ellen Prime
California

DOUG'S STORY
"Recovery in Progress"

Learning to live with an obsessive-compulsive disorder related illness called Body Dysmorphic Disorder has been a significant ordeal. It has taken me so many places and I have seen so many, many faces trying to get help for this stubborn disorder. At times I have wondered if this would go on and on and contaminate my whole future on a daily basis. But I have also resolved that I want to have a life, I want to be able to live as "normal" a life as possible. And to that, I will explain what exactly I mean.

I grew up in a small Kansas town, the second son of four children. My father and mother were, and still are, wonderful parents and really encouraged my childhood and years into adolescence. During those years I realized I strove for excellence in most things I was involved in. My sensitive personality mixed with a desire for excellence started me on a road that I will never forget.

It wasn't until I was 25 years old that I was specifically given the diagnosis Body Dysmorphic Disorder. To clarify, OCD and BDD are kissing cousins as felt by authorities in the field. I was diagnosed OCD for three or four years as the primary reason for my struggles. OCD is getting to be a heightened awareness disorder, but how many have heard of Body Dysmorphic Disorder? I had not and nobody I knew had. In lay person's terms, Body Dysmorphic Disorder is "imagined ugliness" or, I feel for me, "imagined imperfections" is the more appropriate phrase. In terms more applicable to my situation, it means thinking that certain body features such as my hair, my face, my teeth, and whatever other thing it wanted to dwell on, were imperfect. "There is something wrong with these features," I thought; but in reality there was not. I thought, "I will get better if I can find some cosmetic or surface change that will make them look better." Did this pattern of thinking really work? No, not at all. In fact, doctors who work in this area of treatment would tell you that looking for surface changes only keeps the cycle of thinking fueled more and it will make things possibly worse. The reality that I could not be fixed on the outside, but rather had to be fixed on the inside, was a stark realization that caused me a lot of grief, struggles, yet gave me some hope. I feel I am pretty aware of what it means to need to accept something for what it is, rather than fight it and keep beating a half dead horse. But, oh how hard that realization is to accept and apply.

My senior year in high school proved to be a pivotal time in my life up until then. I decided to go to a Bible school in faraway Canada for my college experience. In retrospect, I realize I put so much pressure on myself to excel and be a "perfect image" guy, that the anxiety symptoms really were becoming more and more intense. To be as brief as I can, my first two years of college really were when the seeds of anxiety and the body symptoms started to grow and feel like they wanted to take me over. I managed to get through those two years, but not without physical, mental and emotional repercussions. I tried to alter my eyebrows, my hairline, and hairstyle as discreetly as I could so as not to be too noticeable, but yet look better. My doing these minor alterations eventually led to guilt and waves of depression.

I returned home to Kansas and enrolled in a small Christian college. For the next months and years, I was playing a heightened game of trying to survive. Survival for me was like checking from one bathroom or other reflection to another during the course of the day, while trying to maintain composure as a leader on the campus. I was pretty successful at masking my insides and did in fact get a college degree in elementary education.

After completing college, the thoughts and feeling of "I can't put up with this any more, I've got to go for help" were the dominant thoughts I was having. My parents and girlfriend also realized by now that it was time for more focused, formal treatment and help for this debilitating disorder.

Over the course of the next six years, I went all over the Midwest to treatment facilities, doctors and counselors. I won't mention any of the facilities for confidentiality's sake, but most were safety houses for my increased depression and hopeless thought pattersn. However, I did voluntarily admit myself to three different kinds of therapy facilities. The first type was individual and group psychotherapy. I realized after a while that this was not helping my body symptoms and thoughts at all. Delving into my past in a psychoanalytic fashion did nothing for my most frustrating problems, which continued to be thoughts and feelings about my body features. The next therapy was drug therapy. I have voluntarily tried at least 20 drugs in hope that they would help or cure me. The other therapy was behavioral and cognitive. I can safely say that the last two therapies mentioned have been the most effective for my struggles. However, trying to find the right combination of drugs and the right behavioral and cognitive therapy for me has, in a lot of ways, been like trying to find a needle in a haystack. At least that is how I feel. I feel very fortunate to have been able to try many things and have the resources to do so. But it has been still a very frustrating and agonizing response at times. I have wanted so badly to get better, so we would try this therapy and that therapy, but only realizing that they were not helping. To a degree, drug and cognitive/behavioral therapy has indeed been the most effective. There are two in-patient units I know of in the country that deal with OCD related disorders. I have spent substantial time at both of them. I am not going to highlight anybody here, but the east coast units were indeed very helpful.

I am 28 years old now and soon will be getting married. I have learned so much, as one can imagine. Being exposed to treatment situations as I have has meant that I have had to let a lot of the anger and frustration go. Being treated for these kinds of problems has inevitably found me wanting to find a cure for this. I have thought for many years if I can just find the right therapy, my life will be back in order. Well, I am here to say that there are not any quick fixes out there. If somebody tells you there is one, I would want to check this person's motives. I have been to experts in this field, and I have been helped a lot. I want to say that I am not suggesting passive response here. In fact, I am supporting the complete opposite. I have searched long and hard, remained aggressive with hopes of help, and I am doing much better than if I did not have this attitude.

I would like to put these disorders in perspective. They are tough. They bite and scratch and claw. But that does not mean we have to be defeated. No way. I believe in a wide open approach to living—with positiveness, humor, and hard work as a person's helpful responses. I encourage anyone who wants to get perspective on their OCD illness to evaluate their lives, the dignity and the reality of them, and put together a plan that puts your best interests for your health in the forefront. Learning to shed some or all of the emotional baggage that comes with having a tough disorder is a big step to recovery. I believe in recovery. I believe in living in recovery.

Thanks for letting me share.

Doug H.
Kansas

SUSIE'S STORY

I don't know where or how to start. My name is Susie, and I'm a grateful recovering obsessive-compulsive food addict; co-dependent; adult-child (of an alcoholic); incest survivor; and a lot of other things! So much has been happening, so fast, since the first of the year, that my head is whirling most of the time; and much of the time I feel overwhelmed, and wonder what I've gotten myself into! But there is no desire at all to go back to what I used to be. I used to be a scared, inferior, unworthy, suicidal anexoric. I've been in therapy some 32 years, and really NO ONE picked up on what (I feel now) was at the root of the whole mess. I didn't even feel like a human being—more like a human doing, and never feeling good enough, nor as if I'd done enough to make myself acceptable to you. And never feeling as if I could get everything done that I wanted to.

I'd rush in home with a stack of things that I wanted to get done and make a pile, but before I could get that finished (there were several stacks already around from previous days!), I'd fall into bed, exhausted, and then another day had to be faced the next morning and dealt with—and ANOTHER STACK! There was a lot of fear for what I was becoming. Sometimes, I have been in tears, so disgusted with myself, frustrated and feeling disgusted, and not knowing where to turn; and that is when life gets to be too much. I couldn't go on living as I was in so much pain and confusion. I've tried to end my life three or four times. But God had different plans for me.

God has led me through some mighty dark tunnels and dungeons, but never left me alone to face the demons by myself, even though a lot of times, I've felt so completely worthless and alone. I do sincerely believe, trust, and know that He has provided the steps I've needed to take all my life, preparing me with each one for the next chapter to be revealed. My self-esteem has increased a million per cent, and I can truly mean it when I say, "I love me!" He is guiding me every day, and my life is becoming a lot more harmonious and peaceful; even the stacks around me are looking smaller!

I must also give credit to a medication (Anafranil) that I feel has really opened the door for me. I don't know why or how it works, but I am very grateful. I forgot to mention, I am an RN, and have been to graduate school. But, through it all, I was so full of self-hate and guilt that I couldn't stand myself. I studied all the time (harder than most others—in the upper 10% of the class at graduation) and really couldn't relax and enjoy myself in any of it. Recently, we had a 40-year reunion, and I felt 1000% better than I did at graduation; and I could share and feel a part of the group.

I am now forming a self-help OCA support group because I want to share my recovery and the promises of OCA with others who are still suffering. To know the freedom and the peace of mind that come with losing the self-pity and shame. The insecurities and fears will lessen, and they'll welcome change. The constant struggles will be relieved and they'll surely know that God is doing for them what they couldn't do for themselves!

Susie S.
Jonesboro, Arkansas

120

"And ever since that," the Hatter went on in a mournful tone, *"he won't do a thing I ask! It's always six o'clock now."*

Lewis Carroll

Trapped as effectively as a rat in a trap...

Daily, running in circles...endless, repetitive, incomplete, never quite finished circles.

Trapped like a rat...

Hour after hour after hour of sameness...day in and day out. Days of the week meaning nothing, all the same pattern.

Trapped like a rat...

A wonderful house with 11 big rooms...but only eight of the 11 are "safe" to go into as these are cleaned each day. No energy is left over to make the other three rooms "safe."

Trapped like a rat...

The incredible WANTING to be able to simply walk freely through my own house...without being afraid, without worrying about accidently touching something that isn't "clean."

Trapped like a rat...

Not able to even remember anymore what it was like to not be concerned about doorknobs, telephones, light switches, handles, etc.

Trapped like a rat...

Always vividly remembering what it was like not to pull back from my children's outstretched arms...to be able to return their hugs freely and ferociously, not giving a damn about dirty or sticky hands touching me.

Trapped like a rat...

Could I ever walk in and out of my house without rituals? It seems so long ago, almost as if it had happened to another woman in another life.

Trapped like a rat...

I want to make cheesecake, eggplant Parmesan, eggs Benedict; turkey with stuffing, fried chicken, a birthday cake with all the trimmings...I want to COOK AGAIN...without being terrified that I've made a gigantic mess...I want to be able to just open the refrigerator door without fear.

Trapped like a rat...

The weighty, guilty pain for what I do every day to my family...the very people that I love the most...the ones that I would unthinkingly lay down my life for...and yet, I can't stop cleaning for them for even five minutes.

Trapped like a rat...

I want all of us...the entire family...to sit down at the dinner table together...to eat and laugh and discuss the day's events...no rituals.

Trapped like a rat...

I need my brain to be able to believe my eyes...to really "know" what my vision is seeing and to "know" it's true...to no longer have doubts about "seeing" and "knowing."

Trapped like a rat...

I want to.. bady need to...take at trip away from myself...just to be "normal" for a day or two...to be, once again, the person that I used to be. How grateful I would be to experience that.

Trapped.

"If I was a junkman selling you cars,
Washing your windows and shining your stars,
Thinking your mind was my own in a dream
What would you wonder and how would it seem?"

Neil Young

CONCLUSION

This world is full of occurrences just beyond the reach of our understanding. Obsessive-Compulsive Disorder certainly seems to fall well within this category. Although real headway in this area has definitely been made within the last decade, those of us who have this disease, and our families, will tell you most emphatically that the advances are not coming nearly quickly enough.

In putting together this project, I have been extremely fortunate to have met some rather remarkable people throughout the United States, Canada and Europe. Through this book, I have become once again truly optimistic and excited about the human spirit. At this moment I am full of hope. Not necessarily because I believe that a cure for OCD is just around the corner, but because of the unflagging tenacity of those who are afflicted with it.

When I started this work, my oldest son said, "Won't it be neat, Mom, to see who's weirder out there than you are?" What I have found out is that we are all weirder in our own ways because of this disease. No two of us are alike in either our rituals or how we deal with them. But no matter how diverse all of our symptoms and rituals may be, there is one very important thing that we do all have in common. We all share the feeling of having OCD. When speaking with each other we often times don't even bother to inquire about each other's rituals and what they entail. We know in our hearts that it just isn't important what we all do. The only thing that is important is that we all know exactly how one another feels. We are able, really, to communicate with just a few words. Isn't it amazing how the simple phrase "I know what you're going through" can truly warm you? Just the knowledge that we are not all alone, as we once thought, in our weirdness is vital to both us and our families. The importance of this communication with one another can not be stressed strongly enough. For it is only through open communication and networking that we are able to give one another the necessary strength and much needed self-esteem that we seem to burn up so rapidly. It is extremely difficult and fatiguing to stay strong all the time—every single minute of every day. Certainly it is not fair to expect your loved ones to be able to always provide that strength for you. But we do have an opportunity to borrow it from one another. Simply by being supportive and understanding with one another we are also helping to fortify ourselves at the same time.

It has been very important to me that this book be an honest account of OCD. We are all aware that "the way things should be" is not always "the way things are." After one authority on this subject read this manuscript, I was told that the overall message of the work was not "up" enough. All of the endings should have been happy ones. Well, that would have been lovely; however, that is now always an accurate reflection of real life; and if you have OCD or live with someone who does, then you are getting a gigantic dose of real life. One of the funniest and, at the very same time, saddest stories was told to me by a man who was recounting having just told his best friend that he had OCD. When finished with the explanation of the disease, his friend turned to him and said, ever so seriously, "I want you to know that I will never think of you as mentally ill." Now that's real life. Here's something else that's real life, too—that man's best friend hasn't been in touch since that day.

"I don't like the look of it at all," said the King: "however, it may kiss my hand if it likes."

Lewis Carroll

I have a suggestion: why don't we all simply stop being afraid of words like "crazy," "mentally ill," "nuts," etc. The words, the labels are not what are important; at best, those words are only umbrellas or wastebaskets anyway. I would like to think that, because someone has OCD, people could get past the labels and just accept them for what they are—someone who has a physical illness but nonetheless is probably still well worth knowing. Consider just how dull, bland, quiet and colorless our world would be if it hadn't been, then and now, for men and women with chemical imbalances. True, the world could have done without Hitler, Genghis Khan and Saddam Hussein. But aren't we better off for having had the likes of da Vinci, van Gogh, Rembrandt, Ernest Hemingway, Samuel Johnson, Mozart, Billie Holiday, Robin Williams, Fitzgerald (both Zelda and F. Scott), Winston Churchill, Howard Hughes, Walt Disney—the list is endless. Also, we shouldn't forget all the men and women who, through their religious scrupulosity and rituals, attained hierarchy and, in some cases, even sainthood within the Catholic Church. Is it even possible, I wonder, to have genius without also having a chemical imbalance?

However, since I don't foresee any hope of our not using labels (after all, it does make us more comfortable when we can put a name on something), let me get real picky here and come up with a more realistic name for this illness. Please, a disorder is what my car gets when it won't start. With a bit of adjusting and tinkering, it can usually be repaired. My brain, on the other hand, has a disease—Obsessive-Compulsive Disease.

When you care about someone, then you must fully join them in their realities and, at the same time, gracefully accept their boundaries. If and when this feat is ever achieved on a much larger scale by everyone, then "the way things should be" will become "the way things are."

"All the joy or sorrow for the happiness or calamities for others is produced by an act of imagination...placing us, for a time, in the condition of him we contemplate."

Samuel Johnson

"PLUGGED IN"

Prodigy has an on-line service software package to be used in conjunction with a modem on your computer. This package has over 750 subjects from which to choose, ranging from archeology to zoo-pets. Of interest to those of us with OCD is *Prodigy's* Medical Support Bulletin Board. This network not only furnishes the most up-to-date medical information, but also, with well over two million subscribers in the U.S., it gives those of us with OCD and our families an opportunity to "talk" with others who suffer and live with this disease. The Medical Support Bulletin Board is offered at a special rate with the express purpose of helping families who are in need of support.

For further information, please contact *Prodigy* toll-free: **1-800-776-0840.**

REFERENCES AND SUGGESTED READING

Greist, John. Obsessive Compulsive Disorder: A Guide. 3rd edition. Madison, WI. Obsessive Compulsive Information Center, University of Wisconsin, 1991.

VanNoppen, Barbara. Learning to Live with Obsessive Compulsive Disorder. New Haven, CT. OC Foundation, 1989 (Guidebook for families available from OC Foundation). 2nd edition, 1993.

Rapoport, Judith. The Boy Who Couldn't Stop Washing: The Experience and Treatment of Obsessive-Compulsive Disorder. New York. EP Dutton, 1989.

Baer, Lee. Getting Control: Overcoming Your Obsessions and Compulsions. Boston, MA. Little, Brown, 1991.

Pleasants, Carol. Trichotillomania: Compulsive Hair Pulling. New Haven, CT. (Available through OC Foundation.)

Neziroglu, Fugen and José Yargura-Tobias. Over and Over Again: Understanding Obsessive-Compulsive Disorder. Lexington, MA. Lexington Books, 1991.

Steketee, Gail and Kerrin White. When Once is not Enough: Help for Obsessive-Compulsives. Oakland, CA. New Harbinger Press, 1990.

George, Mark, Charles Kellner, Mark Fossey. Obsessive-Compulsive Symptoms in a Patient with Multiple Sclerosis: Brief Reports. Journal of Nervous and Mental Disease, Vol. 177, No. 5, 1989. Williams and Wilkins.

American Psychiatric Association. Diagnostic and Statistical Manual of Mental Disorders. Third edition, revised. Washington, D.C. American Psychiatric Association, 1987.

Winokur, George and Paula Clayton. The Medical Basis of Psychiatry. W.B. Saunders Co., Philadelphia, PA, 1986.

Kandel, Eric and James Schwartz. Principles of Neural Science. Second edition. Elsevier Science Publishing Co., Inc. New York, NY, 1985.

Heller, Leland M. Life at the Border. Second edition, 1992. Dyslimbia Press, Inc. West Palm Beach, FL.

Wingerson, Lois. Mapping Our Genes: The Genome Project and the Future of Medicine. New York. Dutton, 1990.

Bate, Walter Jackson. Samuel Johnson. Harcourt Brace Jovanovich. New York, 1977.

Pottle, Frederick. Boswell's London Journal, 1762-1763. Yale University. McGraw-Hill Book Co., Inc. New York, NY, 1950.

Pauls, David, Ph.D. Human Geneticist. Child Study Center. Yale University

School of Medicine. New Haven, CT.

Black, Donal W., et al. A Family Study of Obsessive-Compulsive Disorder. Arch. Gen. Psychiatry, Vol. 49, 1992.

Pauls, David L., et al. Gilles de la Tourette's Syndrome and Obsessive-Compulsive Disorder. Arch. Gen. Psychiatry, Vol. 43, Dec. 1986.

De la Tourette, G. Etude sur une affection nerveuse caraterisée par de l'incoordination motrice accompagnée d'echolalie et de coprolie. Arch. Neurol. 1885. 9:19;42, 158-200.

Pauls, David L., et al. Segregation and Linkage Analyses of Tourette's Syndrome and Related Disorders. American Academy of Child and Adolescent Psychiatry. 29, 2:195-203. 1990.

OC Foundation. P.O. Box 70, Milford, CT 06460 (203)878-5669.

The Child Psychopharmacology Information Center. University of Wisconsin, C.S.C., Dept. of Psychiatry, B6/227. 600 Highland Ave., Madison, WI 53792-2475 (608)263-6171.

Dean Foundation for Health, Research and Education. 8000 Excelsior Drive, Suite 203, Madison, WI 53717-1914.

Prodigy Medical Support Bulletin Board. Toll Free 1-800-776-0840.

Esser, Aristide H., M.D. 21 North Broadway, Nyack, NY 10960 (914) 358-2970. Further information on "A + T" Therapy.

Pato, Michele Tortora, M.D. and Joseph Zohar, M.D. Current Treatments of Obsessive-Compulsive Disorder. American Psychiatric Press, Washington, D.C. 1991.

Foa, Edna, Ph.D. and Reid Wilson, Ph.D. Stop Obsessing! Bantam Books, New York, 1991.

Callner, James. "The Touching Tree." Writer/director/teacher. For more information about booking a presentation of "The Touching Tree" with speaker Mr. Callner, please contact Awareness Films, 435 Alberto Way #3, Los Gatos, CA 95032 (408) 395-5669.

"The Touching Tree" is available through the OC Foundation (203) 878-5669 or Pyramid Films 1-800-421-2304.

Kavanaugh, Philip, M.D. Magnificent Addiction. Aslan Publishing, Lower Lake, CA 95457. 1992.

Carroll, Lewis. Alice's Adventures in Wonderland.

Carroll, Lewis. Through the Looking-Glass.

Dilligaf Publishing, 64 Court Street, Ellsworth, Maine 04605 (207) 667-5031.

Esser, A.H. and S. Lacey. Mental Illness: A Home Care Guide. New York. Wiley. 1989.

"Oh, I've had such a curious dream!" said Alice.

Alice's Adventures in Wonderland
Lewis Carroll